KNITTING Scandinavian SLIPPERS and SOCKS

Laura Farson

Martingale®
& COMPANY

*To Russ for his amazing
support and patience*

ACKNOWLEDGMENTS

Thanks to the following who contributed to the completion of this book.

For their support:

❀ Kay Corey, Margaret Gutgesell,
M. Ann Young, Carolyn Sherman,
and Cat Bordhi.

For their donation of yarns:

❀ Shannon and Jean Dunbabin, and
Stacy Fletcher at Cascade Yarns.

❀ Chet Petkiewicz at Frog Tree Yarns.

For their needles:

❀ Juli Mulcahy and Wendy Zhang
at Westing Bridge.

❀ And this book wouldn't be
complete without the team
at Martingale & Company,
especially Ursula Reikes and
Adrienne Smitke.

Knitting Scandinavian Slippers and Socks
© 2012 by Laura Farson

Martingale & Company®
19021 120th Ave. NE, Suite 102
Bothell, WA 98011 USA
www.martingale-pub.com

Printed in China
17 16 15 14 13 12   8 7 6 5 4 3 2 1

**Library of Congress Cataloging-in-Publication Data
is available upon request.**

ISBN: 978-1-60468-049-2

CREDITS

President & CEO ❀ Tom Wierzbicki
Editor in Chief ❀ Mary V. Green
Design Director ❀ Paula Schlosser
Managing Editor ❀ Karen Costello Soltys
Technical Editor ❀ Ursula Reikes
Copy Editor ❀ Marcy Heffernan
Production Manager ❀ Regina Girard
Text & Cover Designer ❀ Regina Girard
Illustrators ❀ Adrienne Smitke & Laurel Strand
Photographer ❀ Brent Kane

MISSION STATEMENT

*Dedicated to providing quality products
and service to inspire creativity.*

*Thanks to Tanya Mock of Snohomish, Washington, for
generously allowing us to photograph in her home.*

CONTENTS

INTRODUCTION

Scandinavia has a long tradition of beautiful knitting patterns. Many were made popular through the Dale of Norway sweater patterns featured in many of the Olympics. Others were brought to the New World by pioneers and immigrants. *Knitting Scandinavian Slippers and Socks* takes advantage of these treasures by incorporating many beautiful Scandinavian designs into the patterns, which are a mix of traditional and modern variations.

The slippers are made using both Swedish twined knitting and stranded knitting techniques. Twined knitting makes for even designs with more lateral stretch. Thus, this technique is used for the top of the foot. For the sole, stranded knitting with two yarns, one for the foreground and one for the background, makes a firm, hard-wearing fabric. These combined techniques have the advantages of an evenly gauged yet stretchy top and a firm, durable bottom. The construction merges elements of several methods, which result in an optimal combination of twined and stranded knitting.

The basic Scandinavian slipper is knit from heel to toe, beginning with a two-strand, circular, back-of-the-heel cast on. Increases are made at the sides with right- and left-lifted increases, following the heel pattern chart. Once the heel is complete, a half round of waste yarn is knitted in (to be partially removed later for stitch loop pick up). The foot is knitted evenly using top and bottom pattern charts. The toe is completed using decreases on both sides of the top and the bottom of the foot. The tip of the toe is finished by drawing the yarn through a few remaining loops. The cuff is picked up from the loops when the waste yarn is removed. Two circular needles are inserted into the loops adjacent to the waste yarn. The waste yarn is removed and one even round is knit. Here the most important adaptation of the traditional patterns is made. Short rows are worked at both sides of the ankle. (Detail is included with the samples and patterns.) Once the short rows are complete, the cuff is knit following either a chart or pattern. A very stretchy bind off is used to keep the top edge elastic. Because two yarns are used, the fabric is thick, warm, and durable. If the slipper is to be felted, stranded knitting is recommended for both the top and the sole, as the stretchiness of twined knitting is lost in the wash. But remember, you can't use a superwash wool if you want to felt your slipper.

In this book, you'll find complete instructions for basic knitting techniques, including special stretchy cast ons and knitting with two yarn strands by twining and stranding. There's a master plan for slipper construction, pattern charts for designs using pleasing color combinations, and a variety of size options.

As in the slipper section, for the coordinating socks there's a master plan with instructions for variations in the individual projects. Charts are provided for the color-work patterns.

These pleasing projects make wonderful gifts and will bring much enjoyment and comfort to the wearer.

TWINED KNITTING SIMPLIFIED

❀ Twined knitting uses two strands knit separately; the strands may be the same or different colors.

❀ Casting on uses both strands.

❀ Twined knitting projects are usually worked in the round.

❀ Both strands are carried in the right hand and knit with the English ("throwing") method.

❀ Each stitch alternates between the two strands of yarn.

❀ With each stitch, one strand is lifted over the other one, creating a twist on the inside of the work.

❀ Periodically the strands between the work and yarn balls have to be untwisted.

❀ From the right side, twined stockinette stitch looks similar to conventional stockinette, but twined stitches are slightly elongated, making the stitch gauge nearly equal to the row gauge.

❀ The stitches are remarkably even and create a thick, warm, and elastic fabric.

BEFORE YOU BEGIN

In the Scandinavian countries worsted-weight wool is knit on smaller needles than what is called for on the yarn label, which makes a thicker and firmer fabric. Twined or stranded knitting techniques, which incorporate two yarn strands, result in sturdy, hard-wearing slippers. Most of the projects in this book are knit with superwash wool for practicality. The socks are also knit with two strands either twined or stranded throughout, thus they're extra warm and are great to wear with open-backed clogs and sandals. Instructions are given for knitting with two circular needles, but you can also use double-pointed needles.

SLIPPER AND SOCK SIZES

The slipper and sock instructions are written for one size range. For example, "Women's Medium/Men's Small," or "Women's Large/Men's Medium." For Women's Small, work the patterns with size 3 needles, or smaller if necessary, instead of size 4.

There's enough stretch in the slipper patterns to fit a range of sizes. Adjustments can be made to foot length just before the toe decreases by working fewer or more rounds in simple patterns, or skipping or adding specified rounds in pattern charts. Standard slipper width is indicated within vertical lines on the charts. For a slightly wider slipper, work charts from edge to edge.

Instructions for socks are also given in one size as for slippers. Leg and foot length can be adjusted by working fewer or more rounds than indicated.

Selection of yarns used for slippers and socks

YARN CHOICES

The slippers are knit with worsted-weight wool and size 4 needles. The fabric is firm but flexible and retains its stretch for a snug fit. The socks are knit with superwash sock-weight yarn and size 4 needles.

It's advantageous to use yarns with smooth surfaces for crisp pattern definition. Also, the color-work patterns tend to disappear unless you use a very high contrast. If you'd like to use a variegated yarn, consider a high-contrast pairing such as a dark solid for the pattern with a lighter variegated yarn for the background. Knit a test swatch using the solid for the pattern and the variegated for the background, and then reverse. For an example, see the photo below of the Pink Compass Slippers. When using variegated or hand-dyed yarn, sometimes you might need to skip a section of yarn so there isn't a funny puddle of color.

Using the solid for the background (on the left in each photo) makes the pattern more distinct.

Another advantage to a smooth yarn is that it's easier to untwist the strands than if you used a textured or fuzzy yarn. If you use a fuzzy one, it's important to be very careful when knitting the pattern, as ripping out is difficult and usually leaves a trail of color.

BOBBINS AND BALLS

If you use only one color, you can pull a strand from each end of a single center-pull ball, which is the traditional Swedish way. But when you twine knit, the strands twist around each other between your work and the ball. That, combined with the twist of plied yarns, will cause kinking. You have to stop periodically and unkink the strands. Instead of using just one ball, I prefer working from two individual balls or from two large bobbins, because it's easier for me to untwist and unkink the yarn. I put the center-pull balls into ziplock sandwich bags and secure the tops. The yarn has just enough tension at the closure to allow easy dispensing. And the yarn stays clean!

If you're starting with a hank of yarn that's not already wound into a ball, use a ball winder to make individual center-pull balls or wind the yarn by hand onto large bobbins.

Bobbins work best for thinner yarns, especially sock yarn. I pack as much as I can onto the bobbin, and then use a piece of masking tape to keep it from unwinding. (Packing the bobbin makes for fewer yarn ends to hide, though at first I have to peel back the tape to pull more yarn from the bobbin.)

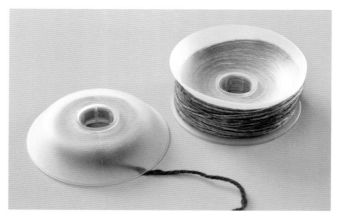

*Large bobbins make untwisting light-
and mediumweight yarns easy.*

CASTING ON

 There are two cast-on methods for slippers and two for socks. All of them begin with a slipknot.

SLIPKNOT

The slipknot is only temporary in twined knitting. You'll start your cast on with it, *but don't count it as a cast-on stitch*. To make a slipknot, hold the two strands of yarn together and make the same type of slipknot as in regular knitting.

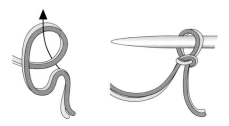

SLIPPERS

Both cast ons are done with two strands of yarn (two main-color strands or one each of the main color and the contrast color). The two-strand version of the circular cast on makes very authentic knit-like rounds at the heel. The figure-eight cast on is easier to do and is also a good choice.

Two-Strand Circular Cast On

Judy Becker has invented a wonderful circular cast on. I've modified it a little to accommodate two yarn strands and use it for the beginning of the slipper heels. I prefer this cast on for slippers, as it makes knitted rounds that match the following knitting perfectly.

1. Holding two strands of yarn together (one each of the main color and the contrast color), make a slipknot approximately 4" from the ends.

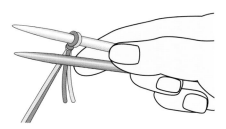

2. Holding two circular needles in your right hand, place the slipknot on the top needle. Hold both strands of yarn in your left hand, with the main color (dark yarn in illustrations below) held over your index finger and the contrast color (light yarn) held over your thumb. Hold the strands in your palm to keep them snug. (The specific pattern may reverse the yarn-color positions.)

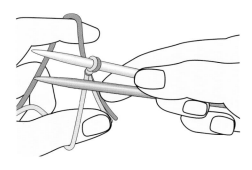

3. Bring the main color down behind the bottom needle and from back to front, and then wrap it to the back in between the needles.

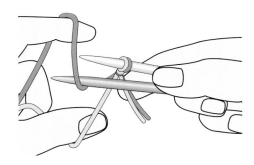

4. Bring the contrast color from the back to the front between the needles and wrap it over the top needle from front to back.

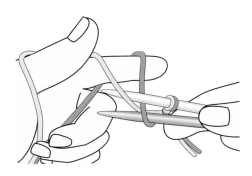

5. Repeat steps 3 and 4 until you have the desired number of stitches. Snug the stitches together.

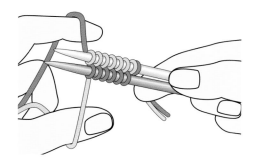

6. Rotate the needles so that the other needle is on top.

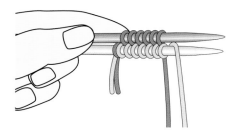

7. Wrap the main color around the contrast color below the needles to secure the bottom loop. Insert the unused end of the top needle into the first stitch of the top needle and complete the stitch using the main color.

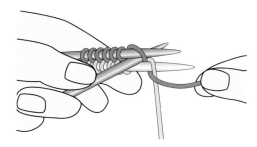

8. After completing the stitches on the first needle, rotate the needles to exchange positions. Remove the slipknot and wrap the yarns around each other below the needle to maintain the stitch loops. Work the stitches on the second needle.

Figure-Eight Cast On

As an alternative to the two-strand cast on, you can use the figure-eight cast on. I've modified the instructions to accommodate two-stranded knitting. It's executed the same as the original way except it uses two strands at the same time. The figure-eight cast on results in an equal number of stitches on each needle. Most patterns in this book start with 26 stitches divided onto two needles.

1. With the two yarn ends, make a slipknot and place it on one needle.

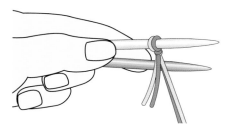

2. Wrap the two yarns in a figure-eight pattern while maintaining the color order around the two needles. Each strand is a single stitch. The dark-blue loop on the bottom needle is the first stitch.

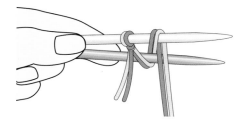

3. Repeat, wrapping six times on each needle. Remember, the slipknot does not count as a stitch. There are 12 stitches on each needle.

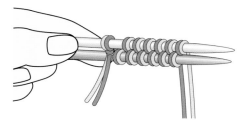

4. To make an odd number, for example 13 stitches on each needle, wrap just one strand around each needle. In the illustration, only the dark-blue strand goes under the bottom needle and over and between the two needles, then over the top needle and down between the two needles. Both needles now have 13 stitches. Remember, the slipknot does not count as a stitch. For an even number of stitches, skip step 4.

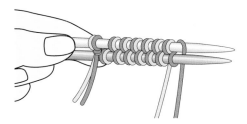

5. For most projects needle 1 (top) is worked in a simple checked pattern, and needle 2 (bottom) is worked in a simple striped pattern. Hold the dark yarn to the back and bring the light yarn over it to make the first stitch in the dark loop. Insert the needle into the stitch on the top needle and wrap the colored strand for the first stitch of the first round as shown on the pattern chart. The charts show the cast on as the first round; the first knit round is above it. Continue knitting with each strand that matches the pattern chart.

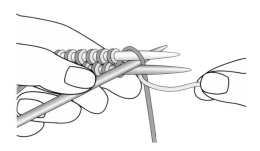

6. At the end of the first needle, remove the slipknot. To keep the short ends from unraveling the work, wrap them around the active ends coming out of the balls.

7. Rotate the needle positions. For just needle 2 on the first round, knit into the back loops.

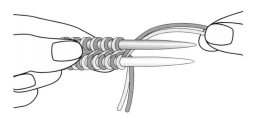

The beginning of the heel when started with the figure-eight cast on will look different than the beginning of the heel when started with the two-strand circular cast on.

Heel started with figure-eight cast on

SOCKS

For socks, the key to a good cast on is that it needs to be stretchy. I like the two-strand long-tail cast on for projects that need an average amount of stretchiness. The twisted German cast on has more stretch and also works well for socks. If you prefer, you can use your favorite fairly elastic cast-on technique and then pick up the second strand of yarn at the beginning of your first row.

Two-Strand Long-Tail Cast On

1. Holding two strands of yarn together (two main-color strands or one each of the main color and the contrast color), make a slipknot approximately 4" from the ends.

2. Place the slipknot on a needle held in your right hand. Hold both strands of yarn in your left hand, with the main color held over your thumb (or as indicated in pattern) and the contrast color held over your index finger (or as indicated in pattern) . This will create a main-color edge. Hold the strands in your palm to keep them snug.

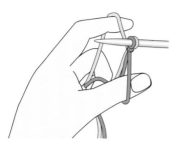

3. Insert the right needle into the front of the loop on your thumb and over the yarn on your index finger.

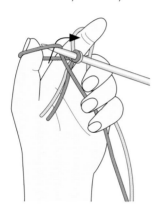

4. Bring the index-finger strand through the loop on your thumb, forming a loop on the needle; snug the strands. You have cast on one stitch.

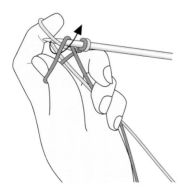

5. Cast on the number of stitches specified for your project. Remember, the slipknot does not count as a cast-on stitch. It will be removed before you start knitting. The yarn that was over your thumb forms the bottom edge of the knitting and the yarn that was over your index finger runs across the needle.

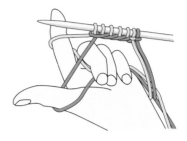

5 cast-on stitches

Two-Strand Twisted German Cast On

1. Holding two strands of yarn together (two main-color strands or one each of the main color and the contrast color), make a slipknot approximately 4" from the ends.

2. Place the slipknot on a needle held in your right hand. Hold both strands of yarn in your left hand, with the main color over your thumb and the contrast color over your index finger. This will create a main-color edge. Hold the strands in your palm to keep them snug.

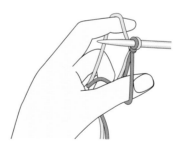

3. Put the needle under both strands of the thumb yarn, and then bring the tip of the needle up over the back of the thumb strand and down through the loop.

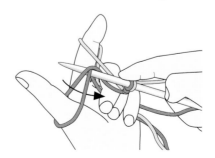

4. Swing the tip of the needle up toward you, then over the top, and through the closest index-finger strand, picking up that strand.

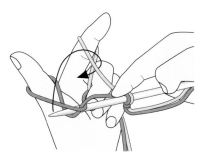

5. Bend your thumb toward your index finger to relax the twist in the thumb strand, and then bring the tip of the needle back down through the thumb loop, weaving through the twist so only the index-finger yarn is on the needle.

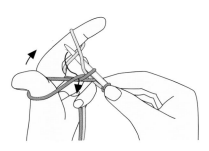

6. Drop the thumb loop and snug the yarns up against the needle. Repeat for the required number of stitches. Remember, don't count the slipknot as a cast-on stitch, as it will be dropped before you begin to knit.

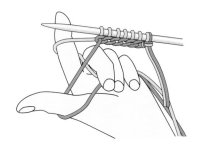

PRETTY EDGES

My favorite cast-on combination looks like a pretty blanket-stitched edge. Cast on with two contrasting colors using either the two-strand twisted German or two-strand long-tail cast-on method. Slip the first stitch purlwise, join in the round, and twine knit, alternating both colors for the first round. Twine knit into the first stitch of the second round. Twine purl the second round. Switch to two strands of the same color and twine knit the next three to five rounds in one color.

My favorite edging

KNITTING IN THE ROUND

Twined knitting is traditionally knit in the round with the right side facing out. These slippers and socks are worked on two circular needles. Usually, I use 16" lengths, but 24" lengths will work too. Recently, 9"-long circulars have become available (see "Resources," page 79), so a single needle could be used for small diameters. Before you start twining, it's best if you're familiar with this method of knitting. I prefer to use two circular needles, but I'll describe knitting on double-pointed needles as well.

TWO CIRCULAR NEEDLES

In this technique, the work is divided between the two circular needles. The instep of the slipper and sock will be on one needle and the heel and sole on the other needle. When knitting stitches on the first needle, you'll knit with the other end of that circular needle. When knitting the stitches on the second needle, you'll knit with the other end of that needle.

1. Cast the required number of stitches onto one circular needle. Undo the slipknot and carefully slip half the stitches purlwise to a second circular needle.

2. Slide the stitches along the cables to the other end of the circular needles. With your left hand, hold the needles parallel, being careful the stitches don't twist around the needles. Needle 1 is below needle 2, with the working yarns on needle 2.

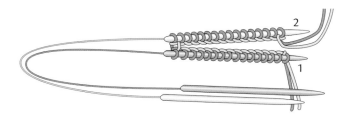

3. Hold the free end of needle 1 in your right hand, and let the unused end of needle 2 dangle. Check to be certain that none of the cast-on stitches are twisted around the needles. Slip the first stitch from needle 1 purlwise to your right-hand needle and snug up the yarn.

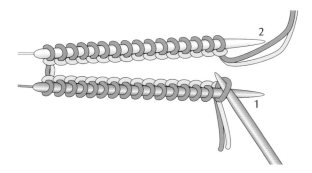

Slip stitch purlwise from needle 1 to the other end of the same needle.

4. Checking again that the stitches on the needles are not twisted, knit the first stitch from needle 1 and snug up the yarn. Slide the remaining stitches on needle 2 down on the cable so they don't slide off, and release needle 2. Knit to the end of the cast-on stitches placed on needle 1. After the last stitch, slide the stitches down to the cable part of needle 1 so they don't slide off.

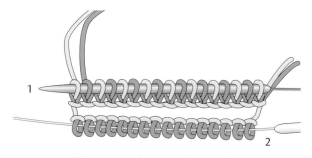

Slide stitches from needle to cable.

5. Slide the cast-on stitches to the left end of needle 2 and rotate the work so the stitches on needle 2 are ready to be knit. Hold the needle with stitches in your left hand with the free end in your right hand. Needle 1 can dangle free.

6. Check once again to be certain the cast-on stitches are not twisted around the needles, and knit the first two stitches on needle 2; snug up the yarn on the first two stitches.

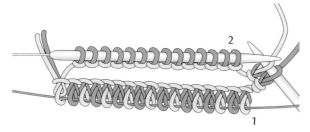

Snug the yarn after knitting
the first 2 stitches on needle 2.

7. Continue knitting around the work in this manner, knitting the stitches on one needle, and then rotating the work and knitting the stitches on the other needle. After the first few rounds, you no longer have to worry about the stitches twisting around the needles.

DOUBLE-POINTED NEEDLES

Some of you may prefer using double-pointed needles instead of two circular needles. Cast on the stitches to one double-pointed needle, and then distribute them evenly on three or four needles. Join in the round using an additional needle to do the knitting. Knit the stitches on one needle while ignoring the rest, and then turn your work and knit the stitches on the next needle.

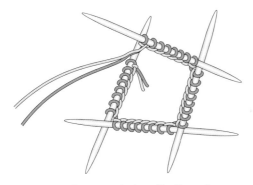

Cast-on stitches distributed
evenly on 4 needles

JOGLESS INTERSECTIONS

When you knit different patterns in the round, there ends up being a jog at the beginning of a round in the new pattern. To eliminate this, at a pattern change, slip the first stitch of the new pattern round purlwise. In the next round knit or purl, according to the pattern, into the slipped stitch. If you forget at the beginning of the round, do it at the end!

The visible jog in the pattern on the top can be smoothed by slipping the first or last pattern stitch as in the example on the bottom.

TWINED KNITTING

The mechanics of a twined knit or purl stitch are no different than the throwing method of knitting. What is different is handling the two strands of yarn and creating the twist between the stitches. As soon as you understand the concept, try the "Basic Sock Pattern" on page 62. I think you'll be surprised at how quickly you master this technique! Then try the "Basic Slipper Pattern" on page 24, where you'll start with a circular-heel cast on, and then continue in rounds.

CARRYING YARN STRANDS

If a pattern has three, four, five or six same-color stitches together, twine the strands every 2 or 3 stitches by wrapping the strands around each other. Be consistent across the pattern motifs.

THE TWINED KNIT STITCH (TK)

All the projects are worked in the round. However, for ease of viewing, the art is simplified to show the knitting flat. As you begin, remember to not knit into the slipknot. Slide the slipknot off the needle and tug gently to unravel it.

When you twine knit, you knit one stitch with one strand and the next stitch with the other strand. The strands alternate every stitch. The instructions below refer to a "front strand" and a "back strand." The front strand comes from the last stitch you knit (the first stitch on the right needle). The back strand comes from the stitch knit before that (the second stitch on the right needle). You'll use the back strand to make the next stitch.

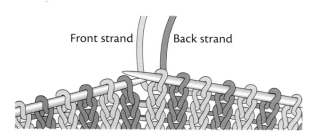

Front strand   Back strand

1. Cast on with two strands of yarn using the "Two-Strand Long-Tail Cast On" (page 9) or the "Two-Strand Twisted German Cast On" (page 10). Remove the slipknot.

2. Hold the needle with the cast-on stitches in your left hand. The working strands of yarn and the second needle are in your right hand. Slip the first cast-on stitch purlwise from the left needle to the right needle.

3. Hold the yarn to the back of the work and insert the tip of the needle held in your right hand into the first stitch, from front to back (knitwise), as in a conventional knit stitch.

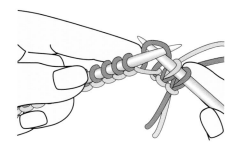

Right needle inserted in stitch as if to knit

4. Lightly pinch the *back* strand of yarn between your right thumb and index finger. Lift it *over* the front strand (blue over gold), wrap it counterclockwise around the needle tip and make a knit stitch, slipping the yarn off the left needle.

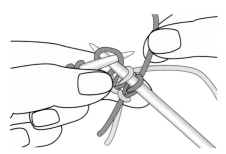

Lift back strand over front strand.

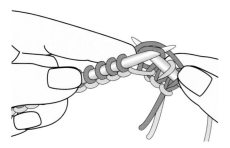

Make knit stitch with the back strand.

5. For the next stitch, the strands switch places, so the stitch is formed with the new back yarn (gold). Make the stitch the same way as in steps 3 and 4, inserting the needle, bringing the back strand over the front strand, and making the stitch.

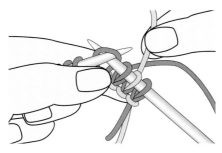

Lift back strand over front strand.

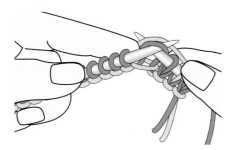

Make knit stitch with the back strand.

6. Continue knitting in this manner, changing strands with every stitch and bringing the back strand over the front. This is what creates the twist on the back of the work. *Always twist the yarns in the same direction, back strand over front strand, when working the knit stitch, unless instructed otherwise.*

7. As you practice, you'll probably start thinking about how to make picking up the strands easier. One way is to use the middle finger on your right hand to separate the two strands. Experiment and decide what works for you.

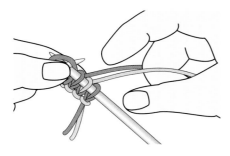

FIXING MISTAKES

If you drop a stitch, pick up the loop with a crochet hook. Pull the appropriate bar of yarn through the loop in the direction of the stitch on either the knit side or the purl side. If you're working with two colors, it will be easy to tell which bar to pick up. If you're working with one color, pick up the longest bar. The yarns have already been twined.

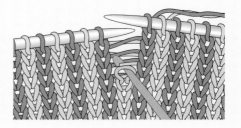

THE TWINED PURL STITCH (TP)

As with the knit stitch, the mechanics of the twined purl stitch are basically the same as in conventional English-style knitting. The strands of yarn alternate for each purl stitch just like in the twined knit stitch. The difference is in making the twist; when knitting in the round, the back strand is carried *under* the front strand instead of *over* it.

1. Bring both strands to the front of the work, but do not twist them. Insert the tip of the needle held in your right hand into the first stitch, from back to front (purlwise), as in a conventional purl stitch.

2. Lightly pinch the back strand of yarn between your right thumb and index finger. Carry it *under* the front strand (blue strand under gold strand), wrap it counterclockwise around the needle tip and make a purl stitch, slipping the yarn off of the left needle.

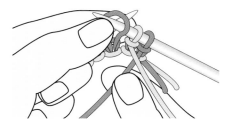

Bring back strand under front strand.

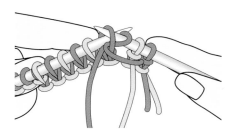

Make a purl stitch with the back strand.

3. For the next stitch, the strands switch places; the next stitch is formed with the new back yarn (gold strand under blue strand), making the purl stitch the same way as in steps 1 and 2.

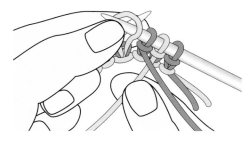

Bring back strand under front strand.

4. Continue purling in this manner, changing strands with every stitch and bringing the back strand under the front strand to create the twist. *Always twist the yarns in the same direction, back strand under front strand when working the purl stitch, unless instructed otherwise.*

When you switch between knit stitches and purl stitches, be careful to use the strands in order, alternating the strand with each stitch, whether it's a knit stitch or a purl stitch unless instructed otherwise. Your knitting will look a lot smoother if you knit the strands in order.

UNTWISTING THE YARN

It is an unavoidable fact that twined knitting causes the yarns to twist and kink together. Untwisting the yarns eventually becomes part of the rhythm of knitting, but there are techniques to make it less annoying.

First you need to temporarily keep the yarn from unwinding off the ball or bobbin. With bobbins, simply snap them closed or place masking tape across the edge. For balls, first pull out a working length of yarn (about 2 yards) and wrap it once around the ball. Make a slipknot and wrap the loop around the ball. Snug the loop. Repeat for the other ball. You can also use ziplock sandwich bags. Place each ball into its own bag and close the top. The tension is just right for drawing out the yarn and for dangling as described below.

Hold the project in the air so the bobbins or yarn balls dangle. Place a finger close to the project and between the strands and gently slide your finger down. The yarns will untwist and the bobbins or balls spiral, relaxing the kinks. Remove the slipknots from around the balls or open the bobbins and pull out additional yarn to continue knitting.

When you make a project, you may shift from working two strands of the main color to one strand of the main color and one of the contrast color for a few rounds, and then go back to two strands of the main color. You have a choice whether to cut one of the main-color strands or to float it up a few rows and pick it up when you're done with the contrast color. If you hate weaving in ends and decide to carry the extra strand up a few rows, untwisting three strands can be messy. Keep the main-color balls on one side of your knitting and the contrast color on the other, and the untwisting will be easier.

STRANDED KNITTING

 Some of the heels and soles of the slippers are worked in two-color stranded knitting. Unlike twined knitting where the yarn strands are intentionally twisted, yarns are kept separate and knit alternately to make the pattern of stitches. There are several methods for handling the two yarns.

I use two hands with the dominant color in my left hand, knitting continental style, and the contrast color in my right hand, English "throwing" style. This maintains the consistency of the dominant color. (See "Yarn Dominance" below.)

The two yarns can be held in the left hand, continental style, with the right needle picking up the color indicated in the pattern. Each yarn strand is kept in the same position throughout, never twisted. It is more difficult to manage the tension, as each yarn is used up differently.

Two yarns can be held in the right hand, English style, where they are picked up with the right hand alternating one strand over the other. It is important to have the same strand always come over the other without twisting. The dominant yarn is always kept under the contrast strand. Yarns should always be dropped and picked up in the same position and order.

If there are multiple stitches of the same color in a pattern, the contrast yarn being carried along in back is woven into the work. (See "Anchoring Yarn Strands" at right.)

YARN DOMINANCE

When stranding, one yarn will appear more dominant than the other even if your tension is perfect. The yarn held in your left hand will be more dominant than the one thrown with your right hand. Because of this, hold the color you want to be dominant in your left hand, i.e., carried under the other yarn, which is in your right hand. This will keep the yarns from twisting.

The stitches are identical except in the top section, the black yarn is held in the left hand, carried under, and appears dominant. In the bottom section, the white yarn is held in the left hand and appears dominant.

ANCHORING YARN STRANDS

If a strand has to be "floated," or carried over more than two stitches, it needs to be carried on the wrong side of the work.

1. To anchor a strand behind the other yarn's stitch, insert the right needle tip into the next stitch. Wrap the float yarn over the top of the needle counterclockwise.

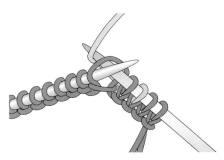

Wrap the contrast-color strand counterclockwise.

2. Wrap the strand making the stitch around the needle counterclockwise.

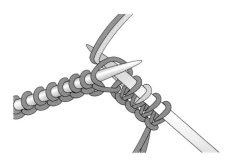

Wrap the main-color strand counterclockwise.

3. Unwrap the float strand from the right needle and return it to the back of the work.

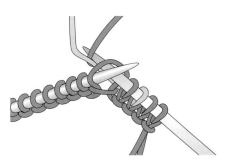

Unwrap contrast strand and hold to back of work.

ADDITIONAL TECHNIQUES

 Here are some additional knitting and finishing techniques that are used in the projects.

INCREASING AND DECREASING

The projects in this book use only simple methods for increasing and decreasing. Twined increases and decreases are basically the same as their conventional knitting counterparts. There are just a few minor modifications due to working with two strands rather than one.

Right- and Left-Lifted Increases

For even and almost-invisible increases, I prefer to use right- and left-lifted increases.

The color of the strand used to make the increase stitch is determined by the pattern, or if solid, the next strand in sequence. In twined knitting, use the back strand. In stranded knitting, use the strand that maintains the pattern or yarn sequence.

For the sock patterns, these increases are made in the stitch right before and right after the marker. The first increase is made with the strand that matches the color of the picked-up loop. On the second increase round, for a checked pattern, the increase is made with the opposite color.

Right-Lifted Increase

Lift the right side of the first loop below the next stitch, place it on the left needle, and knit into the front of the loop.

Left-Lifted Increase

Lift the left side of the second loop below the last stitch, place it on the left needle, and knit into the back of the loop.

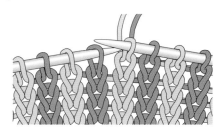

Make 1 Increase (M1)

Pull the left and right needles slightly apart and look at the first row between the needles. In conventional knitting, there would be just one strand between the stitches. In twined knitting there are two strands—one from each ball of yarn. Insert the left-hand needle from front to back under one of these horizontal strands. If you're using two colors, choose the horizontal strand that's the same color as the stitch to be made. If you're using one color, it does not matter which horizontal strand you use. Twine knit through the back of the strand to twist it tight.

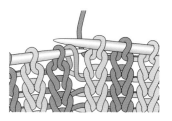

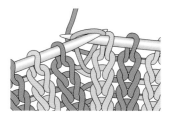

Left-slant make 1 increase

Slip Slip Twine Knit Decrease (SSTK)

Slip the first stitch as if to knit from the left needle to the right needle. Repeat with the next stitch on the left needle. Insert the left needle into the front of the two stitches. Twine the strands by bringing the back strand over the front strand (just like a twined knit stitch) and use the back strand to knit the two stitches together as one stitch.

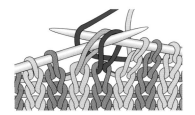

Pick up strand the color of your stitch.
Knit two slipped stitches together.

Twine Knit or Twine Purl 2 Stitches Together Decrease (TK2tog, TP2tog)

Insert the right needle through the first two stitches on the left needle as if to knit for the knit version and as if to purl for the purl version. Twine the strands by bringing the back strand over the front strand (just like in a twined knit stitch) and use the back strand to knit or purl the two stitches together as one stitch.

Twine knit 2 together
(TK2tog)

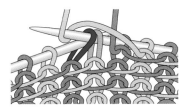

Twine purl 2 together
(TP2tog)

SEWN BIND OFF

This bind off, attributed to Elizabeth Zimmerman, is elastic and neat. I've used it for almost all of the binding off in this book. Unlike knitted bind-off methods, you don't want to bind off too loosely. When you pull the yarn snug, try to match the tension on the stitches below.

1. Cut one of the strands, either MC or CC (it will show slightly more at the bind off), three times the length or circumference of the edge and thread the cut end of the yarn through a tapestry needle.

2. Pull the tapestry needle purlwise through the first two stitches on the left needle. Draw the yarn snug but leave the stitches on the knitting needle.

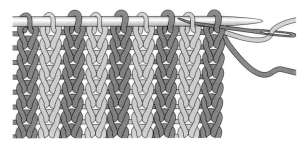

Push needle purlwise through first 2 stitches.

3. Insert the needle knitwise back through only the first stitch. Draw the yarn snug.

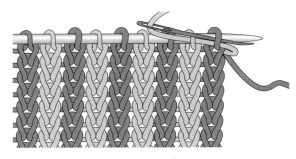

Bring needle knitwise through first stitch.

4. If you're knitting in the round, move the first bound-off stitch to the right knitting needle. (It will be the last stitch bound off.) On all other bound-off stitches (or if not knitting in the round), drop the bound-off stitch from the needle.

   Repeat steps 2–4 for all the stitches on the needle. Weave the yarn through to the inside and hide the end.

FELTED INSOLES

Felted insoles are popular in the shops of Sweden and Norway. They increase the warmth of your slippers and shoes, and can take up some space in footwear that's too big. They're very easy to make. The weight of the yarn and the number of strands knit determine the thickness of the finished insoles. Knit them in one color or in two colors. Use 100% wool that's not labeled "washable." Some white wool won't felt well, so knit a swatch and test felt your white yarn. You can strand knit a tube of stockinette stitch in the round, or strand back and forth in stockinette stitch. When felted, expect about 30% shrinkage from the original knitting.

Felted soles for slippers can be knit in one color or two.

MATERIALS

Bulky weight: 1 skein in each of two colors, or 2 skeins in same color in Pastaza from Cascade Yarns (50% llama, 50% wool; 3.5 oz/100 g; 132 yds/120 m) **5**

Worsted weight: 1 skein in each of two colors, or 2 skeins in same color in 220 Wool from Cascade Yarns (100% wool; 3.5 oz/100 g; 220 yds/200 m) **4**

Size 8 (5 mm) straight needles or 16"-long circular needle

Tapestry needle

GAUGE

13 sts = 2" in bulky-weight yarn (stranded knitting in the rnd)

9 sts = 2" in worsted-weight yarn (St st in the rnd)

KNITTING A TUBE

This is my favorite way to make insoles, because I can knit faster in the round. Using circular needle and your choice of yarn, CO 71 sts with 2 strands and long-tail cast on (page 9). Join in round and pm. For 2-color piece, use a second strand of a different color. For solid-color piece, use two strands of same color. Strand knit until piece measures length shown in chart for desired size. BO all sts.

The tube may be curly and misshapen, but it doesn't matter since it will be felted.

With sewing machine, make 2 vertical lines of zigzag stitching, leaving 1 knit row in between. Knitted fabric can be scrunched to get it through the machine. If it's too bulky, cut tube first, taking care not to unravel edges before zigzagging edges.

Sew 2 lines of straight stitching outside of zigzag stitching. Cut tube lengthwise between two lines of zigzag stitching.

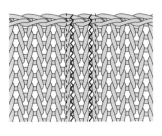 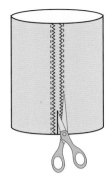

KNITTING FLAT

Using straight needles and your choice of yarn, CO 71 sts with 2 strands and long-tail cast on (page 9). For 2-color piece, use a second strand of different color. For solid-color piece, use two strands of same color.

Strand knit and purl back in stockinette stitch until piece measures length shown in chart for desired size. BO all sts.

FELTING

Many front-loading washing machines don't agitate the wool enough to felt it. Felting works best in a top-loading washer. You can place the piece in a mesh bag or small pillowcase before putting it in the washer. It sometimes helps to add some old *lint-free* kitchen towels to increase the friction. Use hot water, a low water level, and a small amount of soap.

Let project agitate on wash cycle for 10 to 30 minutes; mine took 30 minutes. Felting is an inexact process. Check progress of felting frequently and remove the wool from washer when it's felted to degree you prefer. Rinse thoroughly and spin. Block flat and let dry.

Knitted tube before being cut and flat piece after felting

FINISHING INSOLES

Trace around foot or insole from a shoe of desired size onto paper or cardboard and cut pattern. (Label pattern with its size.) Use the pattern to cut one insole from felted fabric. Turn pattern over to cut mirror image of first insole. Patterns can be pinned onto fabric without concern for grain line, as felted fabric is stable. Just be sure they're mirror images.

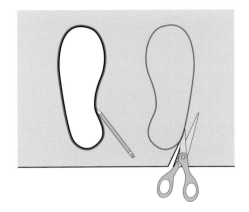

Insert insoles into slippers or shoes. The wool fibers in the slippers and insoles will cling to each other, helping the insoles to stay put.

SHOE SIZES

Women's	Men's	Total Foot Length	Knitted Insole Length Before Felting
6		9" (22.86 cm)	19" (48.26 cm)
7	6	9½" (24 cm)	22" (55.88 cm)
8	7	9¾" (24.76 cm)	22" (55.88 cm)
9	8	10" (25.4 cm)	22" (55.88 cm)
10	9	10½" (26.67 cm)	24" (60.96 cm)
11	10	10¾" (27.3 cm)	24" (60.96 cm)
12	11	11" (27.94 cm)	24" (60.96 cm)
	12	11½" (29.21 cm)	26" (66 cm)
	13	11¾" (29.84 cm)	26" (66 cm)
	14	12" (30.48 cm)	26" (66 cm)

STITCH PATTERNS

 These patterns are used for slippers and socks in this book. They form the background for the charted patterns.

SIMPLE STRIPE *(Even number of sts)*

All rnds: *TK1 MC, TK1 CC; rep from * around.

SMALL CHECK *(Odd number of sts)*

Rnd 1: TK1 MC, *TK1 CC, TK1 MC; rep from * around.
Rnd 2: TK1 CC, *TK1 MC, TK1 CC; rep from * around.
Rep rnds 1 and 2 for patt.

LARGE CHECK *(Multiple of 4 sts)*

Note: Do not twine between 2 consecutive same-color stitches. Carry the yarn loosely and only twine strands between stitches made with different colors.

Rnds 1–3: *TK2 MC, twine strands, TK2 CC, twine strands; rep from * around.
Rnds 4–6: *TK2 CC, twine strands, TK2 MC, twine strands; rep from * around.
Rep rnds 1–6 for patt.

ZIGZAG PATTERNS

When twine knitting, yarns tend to kink and twist together. This is caused by constantly twisting the strands in the same direction. The twisting also causes a slight bias effect in your knitted fabric. Reversing the direction of the twist relieves the bias, untwists the strands, and produces a pretty zigzag stitch pattern.

If you're knitting in the round with twined stockinette stitch, a zigzag pattern can be created by alternating a conventionally twined round of knit stitches (the back strand is brought *over* the front strand) with an opposite twined round of knit stitches where the back strand is brought *under* the front strand.

Regular twined stockinette stitch on the left and zigzag stitch on the right

Zigzag Simple Stripe *(Even number of sts)*

Rnd 1: *TK1 MC, TK1 CC, twining in usual manner, bringing back strand *over* front strand; rep from * around.
Rnd 2: *TK1 MC, TK1 CC, twining in the opposite manner, bringing back strand *under* front strand; rep from * around.
Rep rnds 1 and 2 for patt.

Zigzag Small Check in the Round
(Odd number of sts)

Rnd 1: TK1 CC, *TK1 MC, TK1 CC, twining in usual manner, bringing back strand *over* front strand; rep from * around.
Rnd 2: TK1 MC, *TK1 CC, TK1 MC, twining in the opposite manner, bringing back strand *under* front strand; rep from * around.
Rep rnds 1 and 2 for patt.

Zigzag Small Check in Rows
(Odd number of sts)

Twine knit and twine purl, twining in usual manner, bringing back strand *over* front strand.

Row 1: TK1 MC, *TK1 CC, TK1 MC; rep from * to end.
Row 2: TP1 CC, *TP1 MC, TP1 CC; rep from * to end.
Rep rows 1 and 2 for patt.

If you look at the wrong side of the zigzag patterns, you can see if you've twisted the strands over or under. The twined knit-over stitches look like right-leaning slashes and the twined knit-under stitches look like left-leaning slashes.

Top section shows the wrong side of traditional twined knitting with the back strand going under the front strand. The middle section shows the wrong side of traditional twined knitting with the back strand twisted over the front strand. The bottom section shows the wrong side of zigzag knitting.

Sometimes you may want to add a row of purl stitches for texture. If you're knitting in the round and you twine the purl stitches by bringing the back strand *over* the front strand instead of under, the strands will also untwist. This won't create a noticeable zigzag, but it does make the knitting a little easier.

HOW TO READ PATTERN CHARTS

All charts are read from right to left and from bottom to top. For slippers, the chart on the right is needle 1 and the chart on the left is needle 2. The first solid-color round at the bottom of the chart is the cast on. Increases are made in the second stitch on the right, and on the left side of the second-to-last stitch on each needle. The horizontal row of red squares represents the point at which you insert the waste yarn (see page 25).

The horizontal lines before the toe decreases indicate where to make adjustments to foot length. Refer to the "Shoe Sizes" chart on page 21. Skip the number of rounds indicated to make the given shoe size. The vertical lines toward the edges indicate the two widths. For a narrower slipper, work the chart within the lines. For a wider slipper, work the chart from edge to edge.

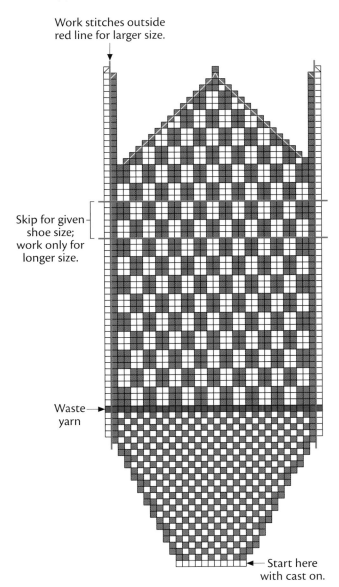

Work stitches outside red line for larger size.

Skip for given shoe size; work only for longer size.

Waste yarn

Start here with cast on.

BASIC SLIPPER PATTERN

This is a basic pattern for making slippers on two circular needles. Several different colors have been used for the main color to indicate the various parts of the slipper. For durability, the sole of the slipper is stranded. The heel and foot are twined for stretchiness and to even out the pattern. In some designs, the heel and foot were stranded where indicated.

The slipper is started at the back of the heel with a two-strand circular cast on. The heel is twine knit and the sole is stranded on two circular needles with increases at both sides. Once the heel and part of the sole are finished, a strand of waste yarn is inserted across just the instep stitches. This is later removed to make the cuff opening. The foot is twine knit and the sole is stranded until the toe decreases. A series of decreases form the toe. The ankle is picked up from the stitches on the waste yarn, and the gap at the ankle is filled using short rows. Once the cuff is complete, the stitches are bound off. You'll refer to sections of these instructions while knitting up the other slipper patterns.

SKILL LEVEL: *Experienced* ■■■▪

SHOE SIZE: *Women's 7/8, Men's 6/7*

MATERIALS

Cascade 220 Superwash from Cascade Yarns (100% superwash wool; 3.5 oz/100 g; 220 yds/200 m) 🧶 4

MC* 1 skein in dark color

CC* 1 skein in light color

2 size 4 (3.5 mm) circular needles (16" or 24" long)

1 stitch marker

Tapestry needle

*Several dark colors were used for MC, and a cream color was used for CC in the sample slipper.

GAUGE: *14 sts and 14 rnds = 2" in TK simple stripe*

STITCH PATTERNS

Small Check (page 22)

Simple Stripe (page 22)

Large Check (page 22)

CAST ON *(MC is brown)*

Using "Two-Strand Circular Cast On" (page 7), with CC on index finger and MC on thumb, CO 13 sts on each needle, or as indicated in project instructions. When making slippers, use same MC strand for heel as for CO.

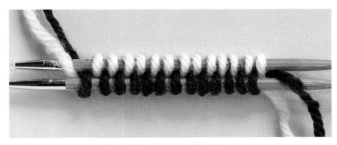

Heel stitches are in dark brown, front stitches are in white.

HEEL *(MC is orange)*

TK heel (needle 1) and sole (needle 2) in simple stripe as follows, or follow specific patt instructions.

Rnd 1

Needle 1: *TK1 CC, TK1 MC; rep from * to end of needle. Remove slipknot. Wrap slipknot yarn ends around working yarn.

Needle 2: *TK1 MC, TK1 CC; rep from * to end of needle.

Rnd 2 (inc rnd): Inc 1 st at each end of needle 1. The RLI is in the second st and the LLI is in the next to the last stitch. Make the increase in the color shown in the pattern chart.

Needle 1: *TK1 MC, RLI CC, alternating colors, TK to 1 st before end of needle, LLI CC, TK1—15 sts.

Needle 2: *TK1 CC, TK1 MC; rep from * to end of needle.

Rnd 3 and all odd-numbered rnds: *TK1 MC, TK1 CC; rep from * around, with the strand indicated in the pattern. On alternate rnds for the stripe pattern, there will be 2 sts of same color next to each other. Second inc in sequence will be made between these 2 sts with the alternate color to maintain the stripes.

For standard foot width, rep rnds 2 and 3, working in established patt until 31 sts on each needle—62 sts total. For a wider slipper, inc to 33 sts per needle—66 sts total.

INSERT WASTE YARN

Using 1 strand of MC (for illustration purposes, strand is bright green), leave a 4" tail and knit across all sts on needle 1. Cut MC strand leaving 4" tail and tuck it inside work. Move these sts to opposite end of same needle. *Twine knit these same sts, alternating MC and CC strands as required for st patt.* Even if you'd previously been stranding, it's *very important* to twine knit rather than strand knit first round of instep. This will make it much easier to pick up and knit sts for cuff.

Waste yarn inserted at end of heel

FOOT (MC is green)

Outer edge sts on instep needle are MC, and outer edge sts on sole needle are CC.

Top of foot is twined simple check and sole is stranded simple stripe.

Rnd 1

Needle 1 (instep): *TK1 MC, TK1 CC; rep from * to 1 st from end of needle, TK1 MC.

Needle 2 (sole): *TK1 CC, TK1 MC; rep from * to 1 st from end of needle, TK1 CC.

Rnd 2

Needle 1: TK1 MC, *TK1 MC, TK1 CC; rep to 2 sts before end of needle, TK2 MC.

Needle 2: *TK1 CC, TK1 MC; rep from * to 1 st before end of needle, TK1 CC.

Rep rnds 1 and 2 for 30 rounds, or follow specific patt instructions for instep and sole.

Completed heel and instep

TOE (MC is blue)

Two sts of same color will fall next to each other; on next dec rnd they'll be knit tog. Work decs as follows.

Dec rnd: Alternating MC and CC in simple stripe or chosen patt, *TK1, SSTK, TK to last 3 sts of needle 1, TK2tog, TK1; rep from * to end of needle 2.

Rep dec rnd until 5 sts rem on each needle, work sl 1-K2tog-psso on center 3 sts—3 sts rem on each needle.

Cut yarns, leaving a 6" tail. Slip 1 strand through rem lps and tighten. Weave in yarn ends.

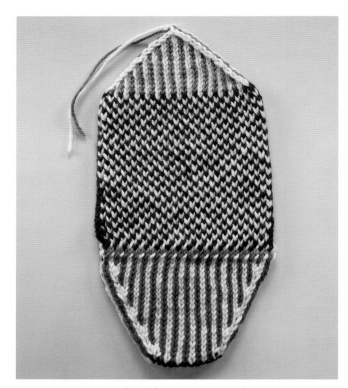

Completed heel, instep, and toe

ANKLE GAP (MC is red)

Ankle gap is worked on sts taken off waste yarn, plus 1 st on each end taken from sole.

Removing Waste Yarn

Waste yarn straddles 2 sets of sts, top of heel and top of instep. Position slipper so toe is facing toward top.

1. Insert needle 1 into right leg of 1 sole st, into right leg of each st in instep, and into right leg of 1 sole st at end of waste yarn. These extra sole sts fill in first *short row* of ankle (see photo at bottom of second column on facing page).

Sole st at end

Instep stitches picked up in their right legs and sole stitch at each end

2. While keeping slipper facing in same direction, insert needle 2 into right leg of 1 sole st, each st at top of heel, and right leg of 1 sole st at end of waste yarn.

Picking up stitches on heel in right leg of stitch and sole stitch at each end

All stitches picked up on heel and instep

3. Insert cable needle or tapestry needle into 1 *middle* st of waste yarn and carefully cut just waste yarn.

Carefully snip center of waste yarn.

4. Pick out waste yarn from middle to each side, leaving 2 sts at each end on waste yarn. These remaining waste-yarn sts will be used to keep corners tight.

Waste yarn removed

Leave two stitches on waste yarn at each corner.

Short Rows

Short rows are used to fill in gap at ankle. Unlike standard short rows, the sts aren't wrapped when turned. Simply twine knit number of sts indicated, turn, and work back as indicated.

Rearrange sts on needles so rnds start at center of heel (needle 1) and center of instep (needle 2). St number is uneven.

Needle 1: 19 sts on heel and 15 sts on instep—34 sts.
Needle 2: 18 sts on instep and 17 sts on heel—35 sts.

Stitches rearranged

On following rows, gap sts will be knit or purled together.

Needle 1

Row 1: Beg at center back of heel, alternating MC and CC in patt, TK across heel to instep, TK2 sole sts tog between heel and instep, TK2, turn, pm. (In this case, these picked-up sole sts may be knit together, to make the pattern work out and to tighten this stretchy spot.)

Knit two stitches past the intersection where two sole stitches were knit together.

Row 2: Sl 1 st, TP4 sts, TP2tog, turn, pm.

Row 3: Sl 1 st, TK to 1 st before marker, remove marker, sl st back, TK2tog tbl, turn, pm.

Row 4: Sl 1 st, TP to 1 st before marker, remove marker, sl st back, TP2tog, turn, pm.

Row 5: Sl 1 st, TK to 1 st before marker, remove marker, sl st back, TK2tog tbl, TK to end of needle 1.

Finished short rows on one side of slipper

Needle 2

Row 1: Beg at center of instep, TK across instep to heel, TK2 sole sts tog between instep and heel, TK2, turn, pm.

Rows 2–4: Work rows 2–4 from needle 1.

Row 5: TK to center back of heel. To even out patt, TK2tog across gap.

CUFF *(MC is pink)*

Basic slipper cuff alternates 1 rnd TK and 1 rnd TP. Or follow specific patt instructions.

Rnd 1

Needle 1: TK to 1 st before marker, remove marker, TK2tog across gap. Resume twined knitting on both needles in the rnd over odd number of sts.

Needle 2: TK to 1 st before marker, sl st, remove marker, sl st back, TK2tog tbl, TK to end of needle.

Rnd 2: TK1 CC, *TK1 MC, TK1 CC; rep from * around.

Rnd 3: TP1 MC, *TP1 CC, TP1 MC; rep from * around.

Rep rnds 2 and 3 to desired height of cuff.

Cut CC, leaving a 4" tail. Cut MC 3 times circumference and BO with "Sewn Bind Off" (page 19).

At ankle, adjust waste yarn if necessary to snug up any gaps. Weave in all ends.

Completed cuff

MEN'S GRAY SLIPPERS

 These neutral-colored slippers are very masculine and will be well received as a gift. The heel and sole are stranded and the instep is twine knit. Make the matching socks on page 66 for a handsome set.

SKILL LEVEL: *Experienced* ◖■■▭

SHOE SIZE: *Men's 10/11*

MATERIALS

Cascade 220 from Cascade Yarns (100% Peruvian high-lands wool; 3.5 oz/100 g; 220 yds/200 m) **⟨4⟩**

MC 1 skein in color 8555 black

CC 1 skein in color 9402 gray tweed

2 size 4 (3.5 mm) circular needles (16" or 24" long)

1 stitch marker

Tapestry needle

GAUGE: *14 sts and 13 rnds = 2" in twined large check*

PATTERNS

Small Check (page 22)

Simple Stripe (page 22)

Large Check (page 22)

Men's Gray Slipper charts (facing page)

Follow the "Basic Slipper Pattern" on page 24, noting the specific instructions for each part of the slipper.

CAST ON

Using "Two-Strand Circular Cast On" (page 7), with MC on thumb and CC on index finger, CO 11 sts on each needle—22 sts.

HEEL

TK heel (needle 1) in small check, and strand the sole (needle 2) in simple stripe.

Work incs until there are 31 sts on each needle—62 sts. For a wider slipper, inc to 33 sts on each needle—66 sts.

INSERT WASTE YARN

Insert MC waste yarn.

FOOT

Work edge sts on sole in MC, and edge sts on instep in CC.

Instep (needle 1): On rnd 1 only, M1, work to end of needle—32 sts (34 sts for wider slipper).

Sole (needle 2): Work 31 sts (32 sts for wider slipper).

For given shoe size, work chart to end, skipping rnds between horizontal red lines as indicated on chart. For larger sizes, work rnds between horizontal red lines.

TOE

Work toe decs in established patts.

ANKLE GAP

Remove waste yarn. Work ankle gap in twined simple stripe.

CUFF

Worked over even number of sts.

Resume knitting in the rnd and TK in large check for 1½ reps (9 rows).

Work top edge of cuff.

Rnd 1: *TP1 MC, TP1 CC; rep from * to end.

Rnd 2: *TK1 MC, TK1 CC; rep from * to end.

Work rnds 1 and 2 another 3 times.

Cut CC, leaving a 4" tail. Cut MC, leaving strand 3 times width of cuff. BO with "Sewn Bind Off" on page 19.

At ankle, adjust waste yarn if necessary to snug up any gaps. Weave in all ends.

Needle 2   **Needle 1**

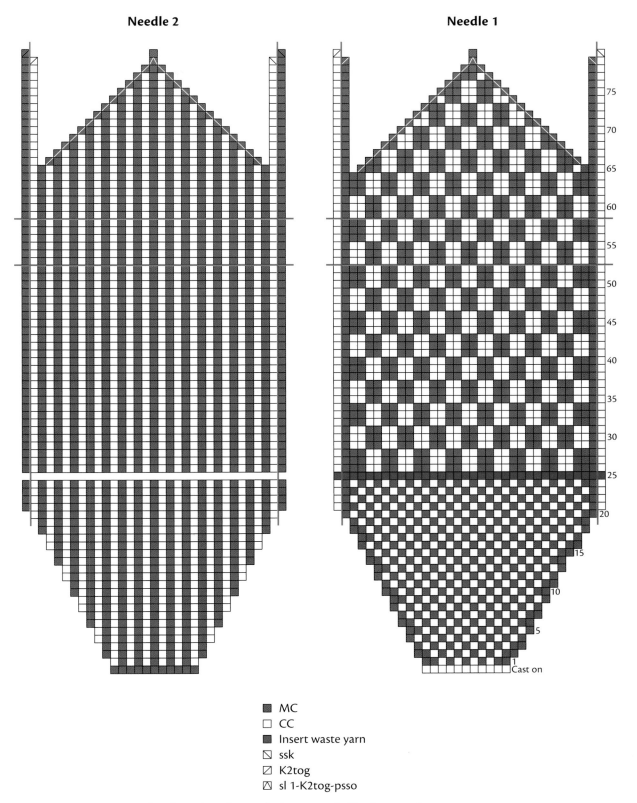

75
70
65
60
55
50
45
40
35
30
25
20
15
10
5
1
Cast on

■ MC
□ CC
■ Insert waste yarn
◪ ssk
◩ K2tog
◪ sl 1-K2tog-psso

For given shoe size, work chart to end, skipping rounds
  between horizontal red lines before toe decreases.
For longer slipper, work rounds between horizontal red lines.
For wider slipper, work columns on either side of vertical red lines.

SNOWFLAKE SLIPPERS

This pattern came from a book of Estonian mittens. I first made it in somber colors, and then realized it resembled snowflakes! Lightened up with a sky-blue background, the snowflakes float on your feet. The heel and sole are stranded for durability, and the instep is twine knit to give it more stretch. The cuff is split at the center of the instep, which makes for a cute variation. Coordinating socks are on page 68.

SHOE SIZE: *Women's 7/8, Men's 6/7*

MATERIALS

Cascade 220 Superwash from Cascade Yarns (100% superwash wool; 3.5 oz/100 g; 220 yds/200 m) (4)

MC   1 skein in color 1944 blue

CC   1 skein in color 871 white

2 size 4 (3.5 mm) circular needles (16" long)

1 stitch marker

Tapestry needle

GAUGE: *13 sts and 15 rnds = 2" in twined knitting*

PATTERNS

Snowflake Slipper charts (page 34)

Follow the "Basic Slipper Pattern" on page 24, noting the specific instructions for each part of the slipper.

CAST ON

Using "Two-Strand Circular Cast On" (page 7), with MC on index finger and CC on thumb, CO 13 sts on each needle—26 sts.

HEEL

Using slipper charts, strand knit heel (needle 1) and sole (needle 2).

Work incs until there are 31 sts on each needle—62 sts. For a wider slipper, inc to 33 sts on each needle—66 sts.

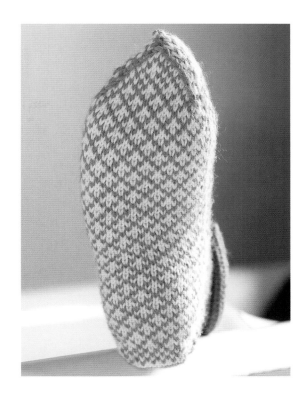

INSERT WASTE YARN

Insert CC waste yarn strand.

FOOT AND TOE

For given shoe size, work chart to end, skipping rnds between horizontal red lines as indicated on chart. For larger sizes, work rnds between horizontal red lines.

ANKLE GAP

Remove waste yarn. With 2 strands MC, work ankle gap in twined knitting.

CUFF

Rows 1 and 2: With 2 strands MC, TK even.

Work cuff back and forth from one side of instep to other, creating split at front of ankle.

Row 3: With 2 strands MC, TK to center of instep, turn.

Row 4: With 2 strands MC, TP to center of instep, turn.

Rows 5–12: Rep rnds 3 and 4.

Cut 1 strand MC, leaving a 4" tail. Cut second strand MC 3 times circumference of cuff and BO with "Sewn Bind Off" (page 19).

At ankle, adjust waste yarn if necessary to snug up any gaps. Weave in all ends.

Needle 2   **Needle 1**

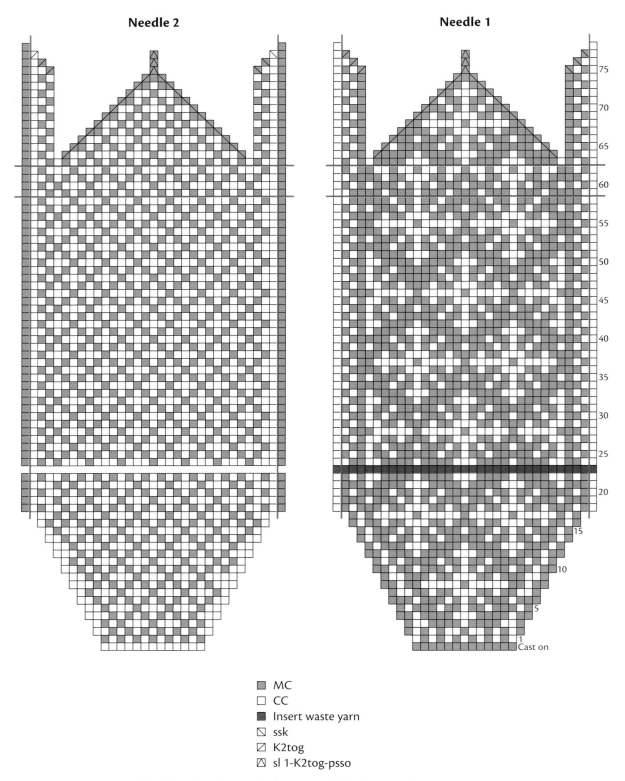

- ▦ MC
- ☐ CC
- ■ Insert waste yarn
- ◺ ssk
- ◿ K2tog
- ◭ sl 1-K2tog-psso

For given shoe size, work chart to end, skipping rounds
   between horizontal red lines before toe decreases.
For longer slipper, work rounds between horizontal red lines.
For wider slipper, work columns on either side of vertical red lines.

PINK COMPASS SLIPPERS

 The yarn position in these solid pink and variegated purple slippers makes a huge difference in the clarity of the pattern (see the photo on page 6). Be sure you make a swatch to test your yarn choices. Companion socks are on page 70.

SKILL LEVEL: *Experienced* ■■■▶

SHOE SIZE: *Women's 7/8, Men's 6/7*

MATERIALS

MC 1 skein of Cascade 220 Superwash from Cascade Yarns (100% superwash wool; 3.5 oz/100 g; 220 yds/200 m) in color 901 pink ▓**4**▓

CC 1 skein of Cascade 220 Superwash Paints from Cascade Yarns (100% superwash wool; 3.5 oz/100 g; 220 yds/200 m) in color 9871 purples/pinks ▓**4**▓

2 size 4 (3.5 mm) circular needles (16" and 24" long)

1 stitch marker

Tapestry needle

GAUGE: *13 sts and 14 rnds = 2" in twined knitting*

PATTERNS

Pink Compass Slipper charts (facing page)

Small Check (page 22)

Follow the "Basic Slipper Pattern" on page 24, noting the specific instructions for each part of the slipper.

CAST ON

Using "Two-Strand Circular Cast On" (page 7), with CC on index finger and MC on thumb, CO 13 sts on each needle—26 sts.

HEEL

Using slipper charts, strand knit heel (needle 1) and sole (needle 2).

Work incs in established patt until there are 31 sts on each needle—62 sts. For a wider slipper, inc to 33 sts on each needle—66 sts.

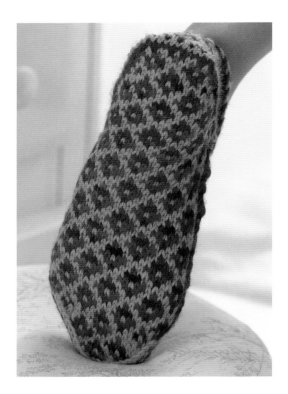

INSERT WASTE YARN

Insert CC waste yarn.

FOOT AND TOE DECREASES

For given shoe size, work chart to end, skipping rnds between horizontal blue lines as indicated on chart. For larger sizes, work rnds between horizontal blue lines.

ANKLE GAP

Remove waste yarn. Work ankle gap in twined small check.

CUFF

Worked over odd number of sts. Inc 1 st in first rnd if necessary for odd number.

Rnds 1–6: TK in small check.

Rnd 7: TP1 MC, *TP1 CC, TP1 MC; rep from * around.

Rnd 8: TK1 CC, *TK1 MC, TK1 CC; rep from * around.

Rnds 9–12: Rep rnds 7 and 8.

Rnd 13: Rep rnd 7.

Cut CC, leaving a 4" tail. Cut MC 3 times circumference of cuff and BO with "Sewn Bind Off" (page 19).

At ankle, adjust waste yarn if necessary to snug up any gaps. Weave in all ends.

Needle 2　　　　　　　　　　　　**Needle 1**

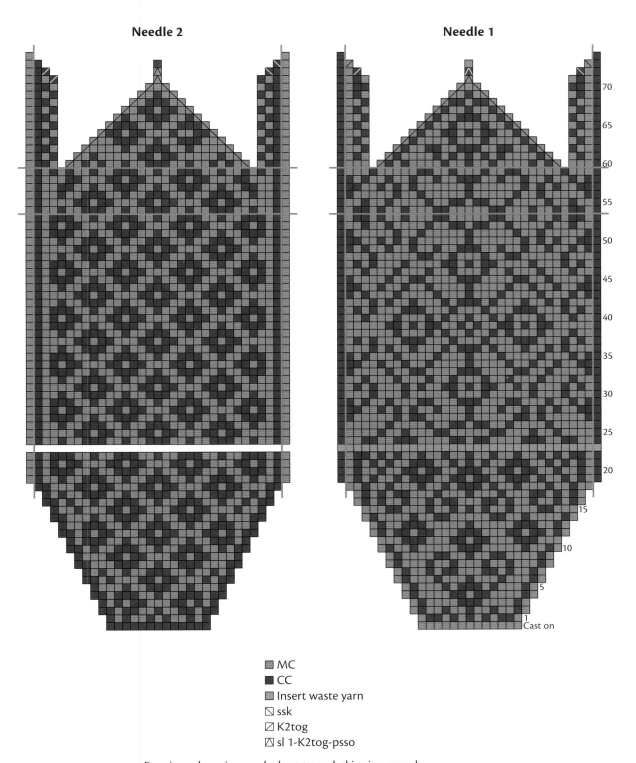

□ MC
■ CC
▨ Insert waste yarn
◺ ssk
◿ K2tog
◹ sl 1-K2tog-psso

For given shoe size, work chart to end, skipping rounds
　　between horizontal blue lines before toe decreases.
For longer slipper, work rounds between horizontal blue lines.
For wider slipper, work columns on either side of vertical blue lines.

WHEEL-OF-HEARTS SLIPPERS

 Your sweetheart will love these richly colored heart-patterned slippers. Make the socks (page 72) to match, and you'll be the love of their life! The large center motif on the slippers is reflected in the sock cuffs.

SKILL LEVEL: *Experienced* ■■■■

SHOE SIZE: *Women's 7/8, Men's 6/7*

MATERIALS

Cascade 220 Superwash from Cascade Yarns (100% superwash wool; 3.5 oz/100 g; 220 yds/200 m) ④

MC 1 skein in color 819 brown

CC 1 skein in color 859 turquoise green

2 size 4 (3.5 mm) circular needles (16" or 24" long)

1 stitch marker

Tapestry needle

GAUGE: *13 sts and 14 rnds = 2" in twined knitting*

PATTERNS

Small Check (page 22)

Wheel-of-Hearts Slipper charts (page 40)

Follow the "Basic Slipper Pattern" on page 24, noting the specific instructions for each part of the slipper.

CAST ON

Using "Two-Strand Circular Cast On" (page 7), with MC on index finger and CC on thumb, CO 13 sts on each needle—26 sts.

HEEL

Using slipper charts, twine knit the heel (needle 1) and strand the sole (needle 2).

Work incs until there are 31 sts on each needle—62 sts. For a wider slipper, inc to 33 sts on each needle—66 sts.

INSERT WASTE YARN

Insert CC waste yarn.

FOOT AND TOE

For given shoe size, work chart to end, skipping rnds between horizontal red lines as indicated on chart. For larger sizes, work rnds between horizontal red lines.

ANKLE GAP

Remove waste yarn. Work ankle gap in twined small check.

CUFF

Worked over odd number of sts. Inc 1 st in first rnd if necessary for odd number.

Rnds 1–6: TK in small check.

Rnd 7: TP1 MC, *TP1 CC, TP1 MC; rep from * around.

Rnd 8: TK1 CC, *TK1 MC, TK1 CC; rep from * around.

Rnds 9–12: Rep rnds 7 and 8.

Rnd 13: Rep rnd 7.

Cut CC, leaving a 4" tail. Cut MC 3 times circumference of cuff and BO with "Sewn Bind Off" (page 19).

At ankle, adjust waste yarn if necessary to snug up any gaps. Weave in all ends.

Needle 2　　　　　　　　　**Needle 1**

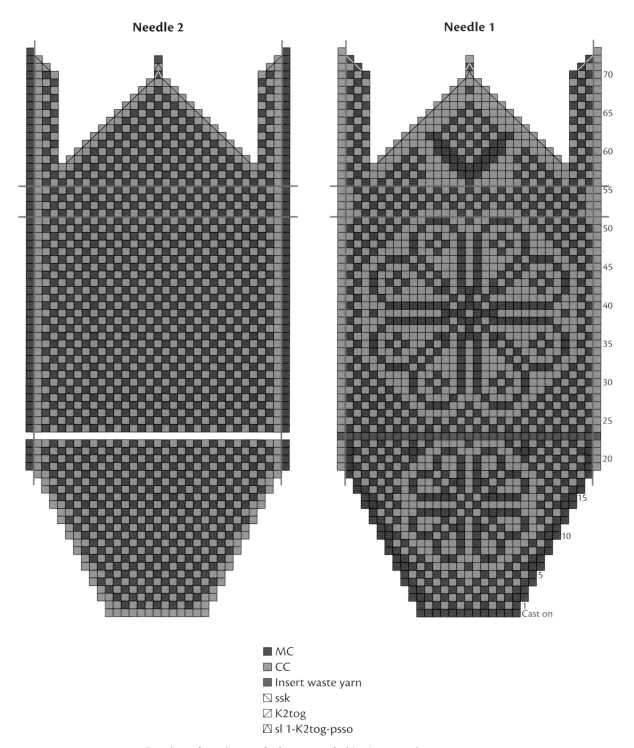

■ MC
■ CC
■ Insert waste yarn
◻ ssk
◰ K2tog
◪ sl 1-K2tog-psso

For given shoe size, work chart to end, skipping rounds
　　between horizontal red lines before toe decreases.
For longer slipper, work rounds between horizontal red lines.
For wider slipper, work columns on either side of vertical red lines.

OPTICAL ILLUSION SLIPPERS

 This typically Nordic pattern is found in many Scandinavian knitting books. Its design is simple with wonderful visual movement. The repeat is easy to follow, and it can be twined or stranded. Coordinating socks are on page 74.

SKILL LEVEL: *Experienced* ■■■▶

SHOE SIZE: *Women's 9/10, Men's 8/9*

MATERIALS

Cascade 220 Superwash from Cascade Yarns (100% superwash wool; 3.5 oz/100 g; 220 yds/200 m) (4)

MC 1 skein in color 815 black

CC 1 skein in color 870 white

2 size 4 (3.5 mm) circular needles (16" or 24" long)

1 stitch marker

Tapestry needle

GAUGE: *14 sts and 14 rnds = 2" in stranded knitting*

PATTERNS

Optical Illusion Slipper charts (facing page)

Small Check (page 22)

Follow the "Basic Slipper Pattern" on page 24, noting the specific instructions for each part of the slipper.

CAST ON

Using "Two-Strand Circular Cast On" (page 7), with CC on index finger and MC on thumb, CO 13 sts on each needle—26 sts.

HEEL

Using optical chart, strand knit the heel (needle 1). Using double chevron chart, strand knit the sole (needle 2).

Work incs until there are 33 sts on each needle—66 sts. For an extra-wide slipper, inc to 35 sts on each needle—70 sts.

INSERT WASTE YARN

Insert CC waste yarn.

FOOT AND TOE

For given shoe size, work chart to end, skipping rnds between horizontal red lines as indicated on chart. For larger sizes, work rnds between horizontal red lines.

ANKLE

Remove waste yarn. Fill ankle gap in twined small check.

CUFF

Worked over odd number of sts. Inc 1 st in first rnd if necessary for odd number of sts.

Rnds 1–10: TK in small check.

Rnd 11: TP1 MC, *TP1 CC, TP1 MC; rep from * around.

Rnd 12: TK1 CC, *TK1 MC, TK1 CC; rep from * around.

Rnd 13: Rep rnd 11.

Cut CC, leaving a 4" tail. Cut MC 3 times circumference of cuff and BO with "Sewn Bind Off" (page 19).

At ankle, adjust waste yarn if necessary to snug up any gaps. Weave in all ends.

Needle 2　　　　　　　　　　**Needle 1**

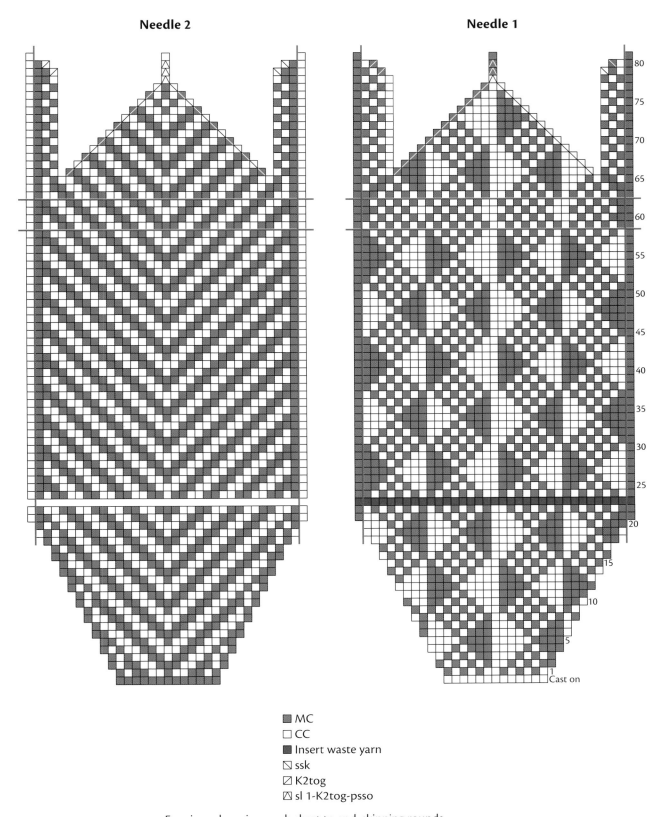

■ MC
□ CC
■ Insert waste yarn
◩ ssk
◪ K2tog
◩ sl 1-K2tog-psso

For given shoe size, work chart to end, skipping rounds
　between horizontal red lines before toe decreases.
For longer slipper, work rounds between horizontal red lines.
For wider slipper, work columns on either side of vertical red lines.

Yellow Pansy Slippers

 Relish spring and summer in these bright and cheery slippers. The pansy pattern is repeated in the coordinating socks on page 77. The heel and sole are stranded for extra durability, while the pattern areas are twined.

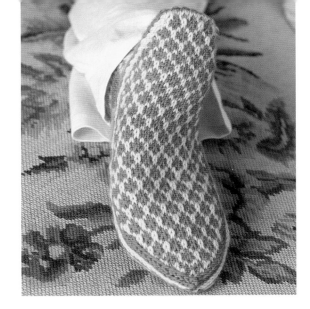

SKILL LEVEL: *Experienced* ■■■■▬

SHOE SIZE: *Women's 9/10*

MATERIALS

Cascade 220 Superwash from Cascade Yarns (100% superwash wool; 3.5 oz/100 g; 220 yds/200 m) (4)

MC 1 skein in color 903 pink

CC 1 skein in color 820 yellow

2 size 4 (3.5 mm) circular needles (16" or 24" long)

1 stitch marker

Tapestry needle

GAUGE: *13 sts and 14 rnds = 2" in twined knitting*

PATTERNS

Yellow Pansy Slipper charts (page 46)

Follow the "Basic Slipper Pattern" on page 24, noting the specific instructions for each part of the slipper.

CAST ON

Using "Two-Strand Circular Cast On" (page 7), with CC on index finger and MC on thumb, CO 13 sts on each needle—26 sts.

HEEL

Using slipper charts, twine knit the heel (needle 1) and strand knit the sole (needle 2), with CC strand carried *under* MC.

Work incs until there are 31 sts on each needle—62 sts. For a wider slipper, inc to 33 sts on each needle—66 sts.

INSERT WASTE YARN

Insert CC waste yarn.

FOOT

For given shoe size, work chart to end, skipping rnds between horizontal blue lines as indicated on chart. For larger sizes, work rnds between horizontal blue lines.

ANKLE GAP

Remove waste yarn. Work ankle gap with 2 strands of MC in twined St st.

CUFF

After gap is filled on second side, with 2 MC strands, work rnds 1 and 2 as follows:

Rnd 1: *TK5, TK2tog, (TK4, TK2tog) 4 times; rep from * to end of needle 2—52 sts.

Rnd 2: TK even.

On next rnd, pm on either side of 17 sts on instep and center back heel. Rearrange sts so that 17 sts for each flower patt are tog on 1 needle, rather than spread over 2 needles.

TK 13 rnds of slipper cuff chart over 17 sts on instep and center back, and in simple stripe over 9 sts between flower patts.

With 2 strands of MC, TK 3 rnds.

With 2 strands of MC, TP 1 rnd. Sl 1 st onto RH needle. The sl st before the bind off evens out the edge.

Cut CC, leaving a 4" tail. Cut MC 3 times circumference of cuff and BO with "Sewn Bind Off" (page 19).

At ankle, adjust waste yarn if necessary to snug up any gaps. Weave in all ends.

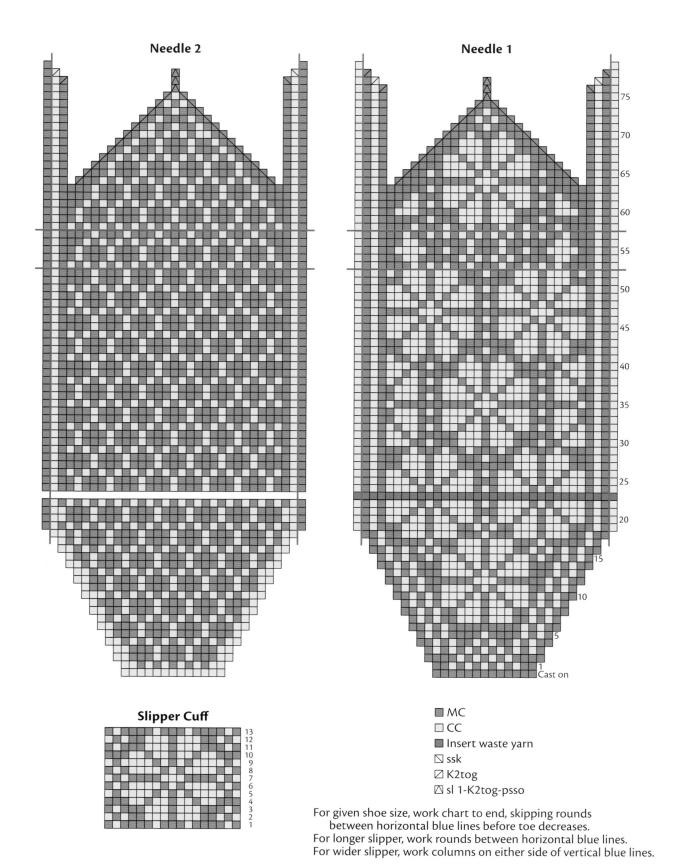

Needle 2

Needle 1

75

70

65

60

55

50

45

40

35

30

25

20

15

10

5

1
Cast on

Slipper Cuff

13
12
11
10
9
8
7
6
5
4
3
2
1

■ MC
□ CC
■ Insert waste yarn
◩ ssk
◪ K2tog
◮ sl 1-K2tog-psso

For given shoe size, work chart to end, skipping rounds
    between horizontal blue lines before toe decreases.
For longer slipper, work rounds between horizontal blue lines.
For wider slipper, work columns on either side of vertical blue lines.

FILIGREE SLIPPERS

 Reminiscent of a wrought-iron gate in a lovely garden, this slipper is masculine in color and style, but elegant enough for a lady. The sole has a bumpy texture. The cuff is braided using single-strand knit rounds alternating with twined purl rounds.

SHOE SIZE: *Women's 7/8, Men's 6/7*

MATERIALS

Cascade 220 Superwash from Cascade Yarns (100%
superwash wool; 3.5 oz/100 g; 220 yds/200 m) ◖4◗

MC 1 skein in color 815 black

CC 1 skein in color 870 bronze

2 size 4 (3.5 mm) circular needles (16" or 24" long)

1 stitch marker

Tapestry needle

GAUGE: *13 sts and 14 rnds = 2" in stranded knitting*

PATTERNS

Filigree Slipper charts (facing page)

Follow the "Basic Slipper Pattern" on page 24, noting the specific instructions for each part of the slipper.

CAST ON

Using "Two-Strand Circular Cast On" (page 7), with MC on index finger and CC on thumb, CO 13 sts on each needle—26 sts.

HEEL

Following slipper charts, strand knit the heel (needle 1) and sole (needle 2). Knit with CC strand carried *under* MC.

Work incs until there are 31 sts on each needle—62 sts. For a wider slipper, inc to 33 sts on each needle—66 sts.

INSERT WASTE YARN

Insert MC waste yarn.

FOOT AND TOE

For given shoe size, work chart to end, skipping rnds between horizontal red lines as indicated on chart. For larger sizes, work rnds between horizontal red lines.

ANKLE GAP

Remove waste yarn. Work ankle gap with 2 strands of CC in twined St st.

CUFF

Rnds 1–5: With 2 strands CC, TK around.

Rnd 6: With 2 strands CC, TP around.

Rnd 7: With 1 strand MC, knit around.

Rnd 8: With 2 strands CC, TP around.

Rnd 9: With 2 strands CC, TK around.

Rnd 10: With 2 strands CC, TP around.

Rnd 11: With 1 strand MC, knit around.

Rnd 12: With 2 strands CC, TP around.

Rnd 13: With 2 strands CC, TK around.

Rnd 14: With 2 strands CC, TK around.

Cut MC, leaving a 4" tail. Cut CC 3 times circumference of cuff and BO with "Sewn Bind Off" (page 19).

At ankle, adjust waste yarn if necessary to snug up any gaps. Weave in all ends.

Needle 2   **Needle 1**

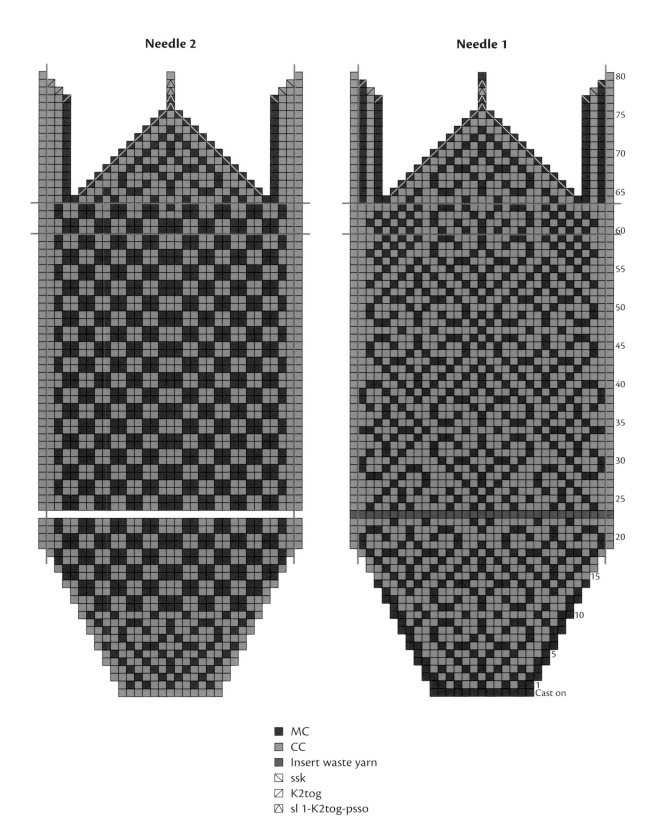

- ■ MC
- ■ CC
- ■ Insert waste yarn
- ◻ ssk
- ◹ K2tog
- ◹ sl 1-K2tog-psso

For given shoe size, work chart to end, skipping rounds
between horizontal red lines before toe decreases.
For longer slipper, work rounds between horizontal red lines.
For wider slipper, work columns on either side of vertical red lines.

NORWEGIAN STAR SLIPPERS

This is a traditional motif found on mittens, gloves, sweaters, and hats. To me it's the most authentic Scandinavian pattern. The whole slipper is stranded—or if desired, you can twine knit the top of the instep. The main-color strand is dominant, held under the contrast-color strand.

SKILL LEVEL: *Experienced* ■■■◗

SHOE SIZE: *Women's 9/10, Men's 8/9*

MATERIALS

Cascade 220 Superwash from Cascade Yarns (100% superwash wool; 3.5 oz/100 g; 220 yds/200 m) (4)

MC 1 skein in color 815 black

CC 1 skein in color 910 cream

2 size 4 (3.5 mm) circular needles (16" or 24" long)

1 stitch marker

Tapestry needle

GAUGE: *14 sts and 15 rows = 2" in stranded knitting*

PATTERNS

Simple Stripe (page 22)

Norwegian Star Slipper charts (page 52)

Follow the "Basic Slipper Pattern" on page 24, noting the specific instructions for each part of the slipper.

CAST ON

Using "Two-Strand Circular Cast On" (page 7), with MC on index finger and CC on thumb, CO 13 sts on each needle—26 sts.

HEEL

Using slipper charts, strand knit heel (needle 1) and sole (needle 2).

Work incs until there are 31 sts on each needle—62 sts. For a wider slipper, inc to 33 sts on each needle—66 sts.

INSERT WASTE YARN

Insert CC waste yarn.

FOOT AND TOE

For given shoe size, work chart to end, skipping rnds between horizontal red lines as indicated on chart. For larger sizes, work rnds between horizontal red lines.

ANKLE GAP

Remove waste yarn. Work ankle gap in twined small check.

CUFF

Worked over odd number of sts.

Rnds 1–7: TK in small check.

Rnd 8: TP1 MC, *TP1 CC, TP1 MC; rep from * around.

Rnd 9: TK1 MC, *TK1 CC, TK1 MC; rep from * around.

Rnds 10–15: Work rnds 8 and 9 another 3 times.

Cut CC, leaving a 4" tail. Cut MC 3 times circumference of cuff and BO with "Sewn Bind Off" (page 19).

At ankle, adjust waste yarn if necessary to snug up any gaps. Weave in all ends.

Needle 2   **Needle 1**

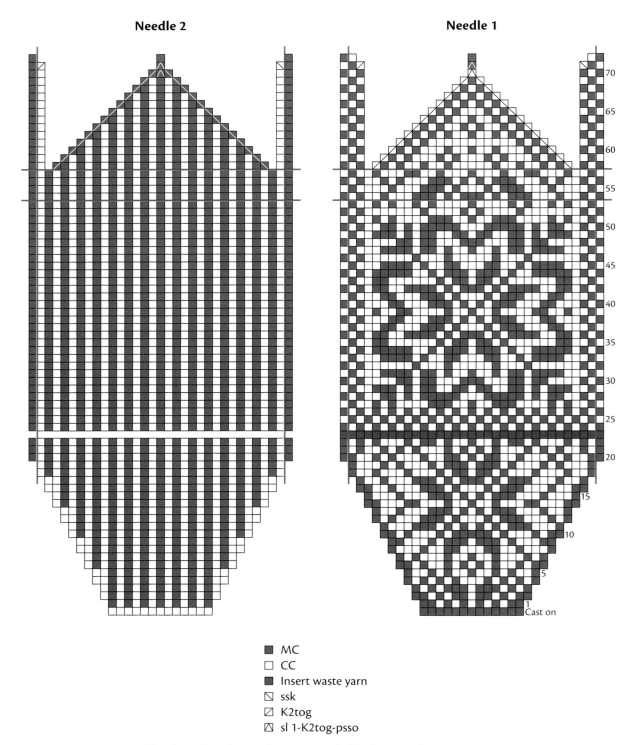

- ■ MC
- ☐ CC
- ■ Insert waste yarn
- ◺ ssk
- ◿ K2tog
- ◸ sl 1-K2tog-psso

For given shoe size, work chart to end, skipping rounds
   between horizontal red lines before toe decreases.
For longer slipper, work rounds between horizontal red lines.
For wider slipper, work columns on either side of vertical red lines.

ELABORATE NORWEGIAN STAR SLIPPERS

 I adapted this pattern from a gorgeous pair of gloves purchased at the Husflieden, a hand-craft store in Oslo. The traditional pattern is very popular in these rich colors. The slippers are slightly wider than the other patterns because of the large motif.

SHOE SIZE: *Women's 7/8, Men's 6/7*

MATERIALS

Cascade 220 Superwash from Cascade Yarns (100% superwash wool; 3.5 oz/100 g; 220 yds/200 m) (4)

MC 1 skein in color 815 black

CC 1 skein in color 809 red

2 size 4 (3.5 mm) circular needles (16" or 24" long)

1 stitch marker

Tapestry needle

GAUGE: *14 sts and 14 rows = 2" in stranded knitting*

PATTERNS

Elaborate Norwegian Star Slipper charts (facing page)

Follow the "Basic Slipper Pattern" on page 24, noting the specific instructions for each part of the slipper.

CAST ON

Using "Two-Strand Circular Cast On" (page 7), with MC on index finger and CC on thumb, CO 15 sts on each needle—30 sts.

HEEL

Using slipper chart, strand knit heel (needle 1) and sole (needle 2). MC is dominant when stranding.

Work incs until there are 33 sts on each needle—66 sts. For a wider slipper, inc to 35 sts on each needle—70 sts.

INSERT WASTE YARN

Insert CC waste yarn.

FOOT AND TOE

For given shoe size, work chart to end, skipping rnds between horizontal blue lines as indicated on chart. For larger sizes, work rnds between horizontal blue lines.

ANKLE GAP

Remove waste yarn. Work ankle gap with 2 strands MC in twined St st.

CUFF

Rnds 1–8: With 2 strands MC, TK around.

Rnd 9: For purl braid, work with 1 strand MC and 1 strand CC, *TP1 MC, TP1 CC, alternating CC *under* MC, then MC *under* CC around; rep from * around.

Rnd 10: For reverse purl braid, *TP1 CC, TP1 MC, alternating CC *over* MC, then MC *over* CC around; rep from * around.

Rnd 11: With 1 strand MC, knit around.

Cut CC, leaving a 4" tail. Cut MC 3 times circumference of cuff and BO with "Sewn Bind Off" (page 19).

At ankle, adjust waste yarn if necessary to snug up any gaps. Weave in all ends.

Needle 2   **Needle 1**

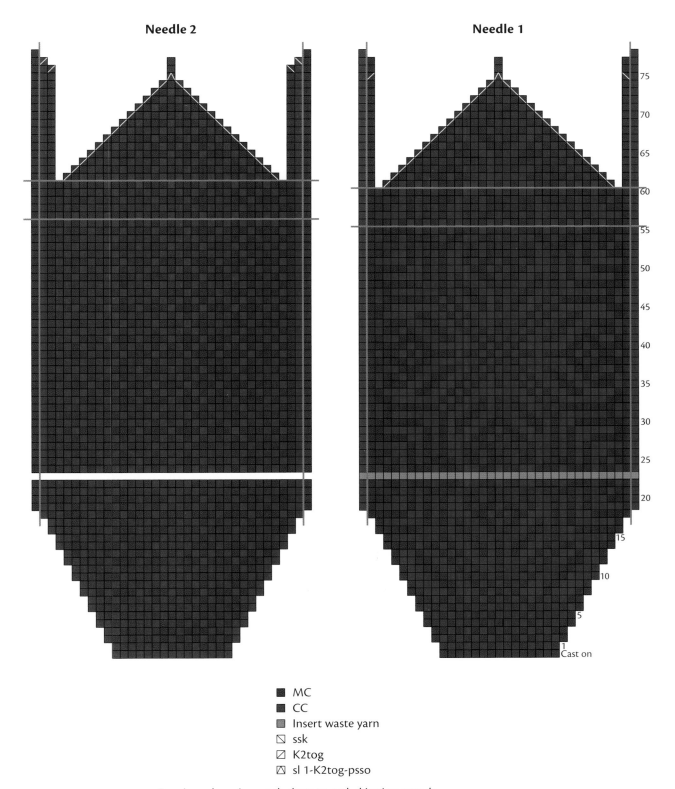

75
70
65
60
55
50
45
40
35
30
25
20
15
10
5
1
Cast on

■ MC
■ CC
■ Insert waste yarn
◨ ssk
◩ K2tog
◪ sl 1-K2tog-psso

For given shoe size, work chart to end, skipping rounds
between horizontal blue lines before toe decreases.
For longer slipper, work rounds between horizontal blue lines.
For wider slipper, work columns on either side of vertical blue lines.

FOLK-ART SQUIRREL SLIPPERS

 When I saw these motifs, I immediately thought of the folk paintings in Scandinavia featuring rough-hewn log houses with beams decorated in rosemaling (folk-painted tulips and daisies), gnomes wandering the dark woods, and trolls peeking out from hollowed-out trees.

SKILL LEVEL: *Experienced* ■■■■

SHOE SIZE: *Women's 7/8, Men's 6/7*

MATERIALS

Cascade 220 Superwash from Cascade Yarns (100% superwash wool; 3.5 oz/100 g; 220 yds/200 m) ⓵

A	1 skein in color 873 taupe
B	1 skein in color 865 green
C	1 skein in color 863 brown
D	1 skein in color 809 red

2 size 4 (3.5 mm) circular needles (16" or 24" long)

1 stitch marker

Tapestry needle

GAUGE: *13 sts and 14 rnds = 2" in stranded knitting*

PATTERNS

Folk-Art Squirrel Slipper charts (page 58)

Follow the "Basic Slipper Pattern" on page 24, noting the specific instructions for each part of the slipper.

CAST ON

Using "Two-Strand Circular Cast On" (page 7), with A on index finger and B on thumb, CO 13 sts on each needle—26 sts.

HEEL

Using slipper charts, strand knit heel (needle 1) and sole (needle 2). When changing colors, leave 4" tail on cut yarn.

Work incs until there are 31 sts on each needle—62 sts. For a wider slipper, inc to 33 sts on each needle—66 sts.

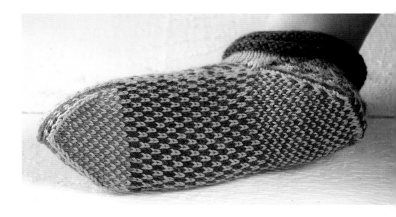

INSERT WASTE YARN

Insert A waste yarn.

FOOT AND TOE

For given shoe size, work chart to end, skipping rnds between horizontal blue lines as indicated on chart. For larger sizes, work rnds between horizontal blue lines.

ANKLE GAP

Remove waste yarn. With 2 strands A, work ankle gap in twined St st.

CUFF

Rnds 1–5: With 2 strands A, TK around.

Rnd 6: With 1 strand B, knit.

Rnds 7–9: Purl.

Rnds 10–12: Knit.

Rnds 13–18: Rep rnds 7–12.

Rnds 19–21: Rep rnds 7–9.

Cut B 3 times circumference of cuff and BO with "Sewn Bind Off" (page 19).

At ankle, adjust waste yarn if necessary to snug up any gaps. Weave in all ends.

Needle 2 **Needle 1**

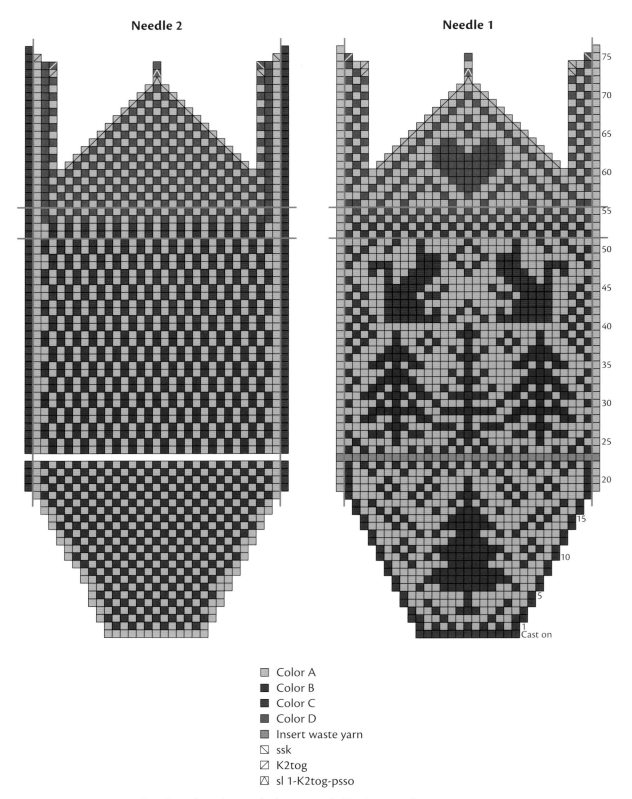

- ⬜ Color A
- ⬛ Color B
- ⬛ Color C
- ⬛ Color D
- ⬛ Insert waste yarn
- ◹ ssk
- ◺ K2tog
- ◿ sl 1-K2tog-psso

For given shoe size, work chart to end, skipping rounds
   between horizontal blue lines before toe decreases.
For longer slipper, work rounds between horizontal blue lines.
For wider slipper, work columns on either side of vertical blue lines.

FOLK-ART FLOWER SLIPPERS

 This design is derived from decorative Scandinavian painting. The tulip with ivy vines is a very common motif, often painted on wooden bowls and on brides' hope chests.

SKILL LEVEL: *Experienced* ◣◼◼◻

SHOE SIZE: *Women's 7/8, Men's 6/7*

MATERIALS

Cascade 220 Superwash from Cascade Yarns (100%
  superwash wool; 3.5 oz/100 g; 220 yds/200 m) (**4**)

MC 1 skein in color 1924 dark blue

CC 1 skein in color 846 medium blue

2 size 4 (3.5 mm) circular needles (16" or 24" long)

1 stitch marker

Tapestry needle

GAUGE: *13 sts and 14 rnds = 2" in stranded knitting*

PATTERNS

Folk-Art Flower Slipper charts (facing page)

Small Check (page 22)

*Follow the "Basic Slipper Pattern" on page 24, noting
the specific instructions for each part of the slipper.*

CAST ON

Using "Two-Strand Circular Cast On" (page 7), with
  MC on index finger and CC on thumb, CO 13 sts on
  each needle—26 sts.

HEEL

Using slipper charts, strand knit heel (needle 1) and sole
  (needle 2).

Work incs until there are 31 sts on each needle—62 sts.
  For a wider slipper, inc to 33 sts on each needle—
  66 sts.

INSERT WASTE YARN

Insert CC waste yarn.

FOOT AND TOE

For given shoe size, work chart to end, skipping rnds
  between horizontal red lines as indicated on chart.
  For larger sizes, work rnds between horizontal red
  lines.

ANKLE GAP

Remove waste yarn. Fill ankle gap in twined small
  check.

CUFF

Worked over odd number of sts. Inc 1 st in first rnd if
  necessary for odd number.

Rnds 1–7: TK in small check.

Rnd 8: With MC over, TP1 MC, *TP1 CC, TP1 MC; rep
  from * around.

Rnd 9: With 1 strand MC, knit.

Rnd 10: With 1 strand MC, purl.

Rnd 11: With MC under, TP1 MC, *TP1 CC, TP1 MC;
  rep from * around.

Rnds 12–14: Rep rnds 8–10.

Cut CC, leaving a 4" tail. Cut MC 3 times circumference
  of cuff and BO with "Sewn Bind Off" (page 19).

At ankle, adjust waste yarn if necessary to snug up any
  gaps. Weave in all ends.

Needle 2　　　　　　　　　　**Needle 1**

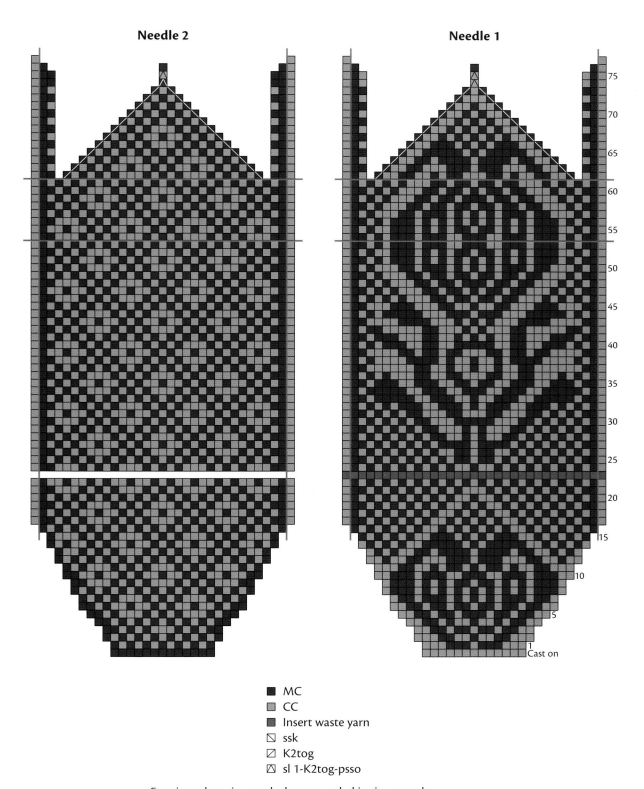

- ■ MC
- ■ CC
- ■ Insert waste yarn
- ◻ ssk
- ◪ K2tog
- ◩ sl 1-K2tog-psso

For given shoe size, work chart to end, skipping rounds
　　between horizontal red lines before toe decreases.
For longer slipper, work rounds between horizontal red lines.
For wider slipper, work columns on either side of vertical red lines.

BASIC SOCK PATTERN

This sock design is the basis for all the socks in this book. It's a basic top-down plan with each area in the instructions defined by a different-colored yarn and a distinct pattern. The socks are twine knit for durability and ease of fit, but they can be strand knit as well. Some coordinate with a slipper design. The designs have an integrated heel and foot that eliminates picked-up stitches. From this basic plan, you can choose your cuff design, ankle increases, heel, foot, and toe-area patterns.

SKILL LEVEL: *Experienced* ■■■▶

SHOE SIZE: *Women's 7/8, Men's 6/7*

MATERIALS

Heritage 150 Sock Yarn from Cascade Yarns (75% merino superwash wool, 25% nylon; 5.25 oz/150 g; 492 yds/450 m) (**3**)

MC* 1 skein in dark color

CC* 1 skein in light color

2 size 4 (3.5 mm) circular needles (16" long), or set of 4 double-pointed needles

14 stitch markers

Tapestry needle

*Several dark colors were used for MC, and cream color was used for CC in the sample sock.

GAUGE: *16 sts and 15 rows = 2" in twined knitting*

STITCH PATTERNS

Simple Stripe (page 22)

Small Check (page 22)

Large Check (page 22)

Zigzag Simple Stripe (page 22)

Zigzag Small Check in the Round (page 22)

Zigzag Small Check in Rows (page 22)

CUFF *(MC is brown for CO, then changes to pink.)*

Each sock has a top-edge treatment, a chart or patt, and transition rnd(s).

Using "Two-Strand Twisted German Cast On" (page 10), CO 60 sts with MC over thumb and CC over index finger. Yarn position over thumb determines edge color.

Transfer 30 sts to second circular needle, remove slip-knot, and join in the rnd.

When switching from TK to TP and back, move both strands, keeping them in the order they were worked.

In the example, MC changes to pink.

Rnd 1: *TK1 MC, TK1 CC; rep from * around.

Rnd 2: *TP1 MC, TP1 CC; rep from * around.

Rnds 3–6: Rep rnds 1 and 2.

Rnd 7: Rep rnd 1.

LEG *(MC is red)*

Rnd 8: With 1 strand MC, knit around.

Rows 9–27: Work large check patt 4 times, and then work rnds 1–3 once—27 rnds total.

Rnd 28 (transition rnd): With 1 strand MC, knit around.

Completed cuff and leg

GUSSET *(MC is burgundy)*

Gusset can be knit with 2 strands of MC for a solid area, alternating an even number of MC and CC sts for stripe patt, or an odd number of MC and CC sts for check patt. Basic sock instep is knit in simple stripe. The sts are set up so that first right- and left-lifted incs (page 18) are made with darker yarn. (Each sock patt will indicate arrangement of sts for this area.)

Incs are made on needle 1. Center 25 sts of this needle will become heel. Needle 2 is instep.

On alternate inc rnds, 2 sts of same color will be side by side.

Rnd 1

Needle 1: *TK1 MC, TK1 CC; rep from * to end of needle, move 1 st from needle 2 to needle 1, TK1 MC—31 sts.

Needle 2: *TK1 CC, TK1 MC; rep from * to last st, TK1 CC—29 sts.

Rnd 2

Needle 1: TK1 MC, TK1 CC, RLI MC, TK1 MC, pm, *TK1 CC, TK1 MC; rep from * until 4 sts from end of needle, TK1 CC, pm, TK1 MC, LLI MC, TK1 CC, TK1 MC.

Needle 2: *TK1 CC, TK1 MC; rep from * to last st, TK1 CC.

Rnd 3 and all odd-numbered rnds: TK even in patt, matching strand to st color.

Rnd 4

Needle 1: (TK1 MC, TK1 CC) to 1 st before marker, RLI CC, TK1 MC, slip marker, *TK1 CC, TK1 MC; rep from * to 1 st before next marker, TK1 CC, slip marker, TK1 MC, LLI CC, (TK1 MC, TK1 CC) to last st on needle, TK1 MC.

Needle 2: *TK1 CC, TK1 MC; rep from * to last st, TK1 CC.

Rnd 6: Work as for rnd 4, except that incs will be RLI MC and LLI MC, which leaves 2 same-color sts next to each other. This will be fixed on next inc rnd, when inc is made with CC between the 2 same-color sts.

Rep rnds 3–6 until there are 51 sts on needle 1, arranged as follows: 13 sts, marker, 25 sts, marker, 13 sts—51 sts. Needle 2: 29 sts.

End of gusset with 25 stitches between markers

HEEL *(MC is orange)*

Heel (similar to a heel flap) is worked back and forth on center sts on needle 1. Heel can be solid, striped, or checked and is formed with short rows. For basic sock, sequence of sts changes to zigzag small-check rows.

Note unique instructions for heel construction using 2 strands of yarn. Cont twining MC and CC, alternating one over the other. At the turns, for first st, use strand from last st made. TK and TP back and forth on sts between markers on needle 1; needle 2 rests.

Row 1 (RS): *TK1 MC, TK1 CC; rep from * to 2 sts before second marker, TK1 MC, sk the last st before marker, turn, pm.

Row 2 (WS): Wyif sl 1 MC pw, *TP1 MC (into CC), TP1 CC (into MC); rep from * to 1 st before marker (first st will be same color as sl st, and patt will change to small check), turn, pm.

Row 3: Wyib sl 1 CC pw, *TK1 CC, TK1 MC; rep from * to 1 st before marker, turn, pm.

Rep rows 2 and 3 until there are 12 sts between markers.

Work heel until there are 12 stitches between markers.

Row 14 (WS): TP to 1 st before marker, sl st and remove marker. From next st on left needle pick up the lp *below* (see "Right-Lifted Increase" on page 18) and place it on LH needle, move sl st back to LH needle, TP this st and picked-up lp tog (yarn color matches st color), *sl lp to RH needle, remove marker, from next st on left needle pick up lp *below* and place it on LH needle, move sl lp back to LH needle and TP the 2 lps tog; rep from * until 1 lp left before last marker, sl lp to RH needle, remove marker, return sl st to LH needle and TP lp and next st tog, turn.

Row 15 (RS): Pm, sl 1 st, beg with strand last used, TK across to 1 st before marker, sl next st to RH needle, remove marker, from next st on LH needle pick up lp of st *below* it and place lp on LH needle, return sl st to LH needle and TK this st and picked-up lp tog tbl with strand last used, **sl rem lp to RH needle, remove marker, from next st on LH needle pick up lp of st *below* it and place lp on LH needle, return sl st to LH needle and TK the 2 lps tog tbl; rep from ** until 1 lp left before marker, sl last lp to RH needle, remove marker, pick up lp below next st and place it on LH needle, return sl st to LH needle and TK the 3 lps tog tbl.

BEGINNING OF SOLE *(MC is gold)*

Join inc sts to sole sts by twine knitting them tog as follows: Work back and forth with MC and CC, purling and knitting, merging 1 gusset inc st with a sole st on each end of every row. Lps are picked up from st below to avoid holes (see "Right-Lifted Increase" on page 18). Using the strand that matches each st reestablishes the simple stripe patt.

Turn to WS, pm.

Row 1: Sl 1 st. Beg with active strand that matches next st, TP in patt to 1 st before marker, sl st, remove marker, with RH needle pick up lp of st *below* next st and place it on LH needle. Sl st from RH needle back to LH needle. At just this intersection, rearrange these lps so correct color faces RS. TP st, lp, and next st tog, turn, pm.

Row 2 (RS): Sl 1 st. At this and all turns, bring far-right strand of yarn (opposite color of next st to be knit) to left and over strand that is in active st and hold it in place.

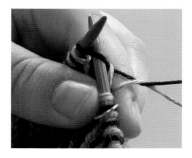

Bring the active strand that matches the next stitch over the opposite strand.

Using active strand that matches st, TK. Snug yarn as you make next st. *TK in patt from * to 1 st before marker, sl next st kw, remove marker, pick up lp of st *below* next st and place it on LH needle, move sl st back to LH needle, TK previous sl st and 2 lps tog tbl, turn, pm, snug yarn as you make next st.

Rows 3–17: Rep rows 1 and 2 until 3 sts rem before first marker, and 4 sts after second marker on needle 1.

Beg next rnd (RS): There are 3 sts before first marker on needle 1. *TK MC, TK CC; rep from * to 1 st before marker, sl 1 st, remove marker, pick up lp of st below next st and place it on LH needle, TK next st, picked-up lp, and sl lp tog tbl, pick up lp of st below next st and place it on LH needle, TK st, picked-up lp, and sl lp tog tbl, TK 2 sts in simple stripe to end of needle 1.

Resume knitting in rnd on needle 2 in zigzag small check in the rnd (using green for MC as in sample).

For some patterns, inc 1 st to make an even number on sole and instep.

Last rnd: Work first 3 sts before marker on needle 1 as follows: TK1 MC, sl 1 st, pick up lp *below* this sl st, transfer this lp and sl st to LH needle, with strand just used TK st and lp tbl, sl 1 st to RH needle, remove marker, then pick up rightmost lp below next st on LH needle (this st has 3 lps from previous purl-tog row, choose rightmost one furthest behind the others), transfer lp and sl st to LH needle, TK MC lp and st tog tbl, pick up right lp *below* next st and place it on LH needle, TK lp and st tog tbl, TK to end of needle. For small check, LLI—61 sts.

FOOT *(MC is green)*

The foot can be plain, striped, checked, or patterned. The basic sock is worked in zigzag small-check rnds. Place removable marker (such as a loop of yarn) at beg of foot to keep track of number of rnds.

TK even in zigzag small check for 26 rnds. Or work other sock patts as established until foot measures 2½" less than desired total foot length.

On last rnd, *(TK1 MC, TK1 CC) 5 times, pm; rep from * to last 2 sts, TK2tog—60 sts.

Upon completion of heel and sole, you'll have same number of sts as cast on. Foot patt may require an inc to make number odd or even as indicated.

TOE *(MC is blue)*

The basic sock toe is knit in simple stripe patt. In order to have dec line in MC, beg with TK1 CC unless otherwise instructed. All sock toes are divided into 6 sections of 10 sts each unless otherwise noted. Additional sts are dec at end of toe-sequence rnds.

Rnd 1: (TK1 CC, TK1 MC), rep to 2 sts before marker, TK2tog MC, slip marker.

Rnd 2: *TK1 CC, TK1 MC; rep from * around.

Rep rnds 1 and 2 until 4 sts between markers.

Next rnd: *SSTK CC, TK2tog MC, remove marker; rep from * around—12 sts.

Last rnd: TK2tog MC around—6 sts.

Cut both strands, leaving a 6" tail, draw MC through lps with tapestry needle, tighten and weave in ends.

Toe detail

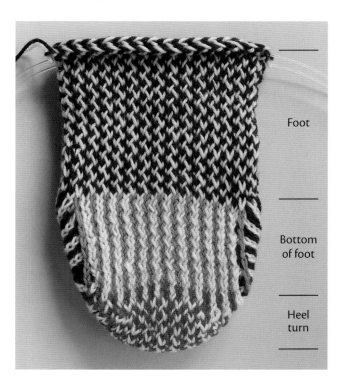

Foot

Bottom of foot

Heel turn

MEN'S GRAY SOCKS

 These socks are a medley of easy-to-knit patterns. Make the socks and the coordinating slippers on page 29, and you'll have a masculine set.

SHOE SIZE: *Men's 10/11*

MATERIALS

MC 1 skein of Heritage 150 Sock Yarn from Cascade Yarns (75% merino superwash wool, 25% nylon; 5.25 oz/150 g; 492 yds/450 m) in color 5601 black 🧶2

CC 2 skeins of Cascade 220 Superwash Sport from Cascade Yarns (100% superwash merino wool; 1.75 oz/50 g; 136 yds/125 m) in color 1946 gray 🧶2

2 size 4 (3.5 mm) circular needles (16" or 24" long)

14 stitch markers

Tapestry needle

GAUGE: *15 sts and 15 rnds = 2" in twined knitting*

PATTERNS

Large Check (see page 22)

Simple Stripe (see page 22)

Small Check (see page 22)

Follow the "Basic Sock Pattern" on page 62, noting the specific instructions for each part of the sock. Entire sock is done in twined knitting.

CUFF AND LEG

Using "Two-Strand Twisted German Cast On" (page 10), with MC on index finger and CC on thumb, CO 60 sts.

Work cuff and leg as indicated in basic sock pattern.

GUSSET

Work gusset in simple stripe.

HEEL TURN

Work heel in small check.

BEGINNING OF SOLE

Work sole in simple stripe.

FOOT

Next rnd: M1, *TK1 MC, TK1 CC; rep from * around—61 sts.

Cont to work foot in small check, or until foot measures 2½" less than desired total foot length.

TOE

Work toe in simple stripe. Dec 1 st at beg of first rnd only—60 sts.

SNOWFLAKE SOCKS

Picture a winter's day with the sun shining and glittering snowflakes gently falling from a blue sky. This is a common occurrence in the mountains of Colorado where I live. These socks will remind you of just such a pretty day while keeping your feet warm and snug. See coordinating slippers on page 32.

SKILL LEVEL: *Experienced* ●■■▶

SHOE SIZE: *Women's 7/8, Men's 6/7*

MATERIALS

Heritage 150 Sock Yarn from Cascade Yarns (75% merino superwash wool, 25% nylon; 5.25 oz/150 g; 492 yds/450 m) ❬2❭

MC 1 skein in color 5604 blue

CC 1 skein in color 5618 white

2 size 4 (3.5 mm) circular needles (16" or 24" long)

14 stitch markers

Tapestry needle

GAUGE: *15 sts and 15 rows = 2" in twined knitting*

PATTERNS

Small Check (page 22)

Leg chart

Simple Stripe (page 22)

Follow the "Basic Sock Pattern" on page 62, noting the specific instructions for each part of the sock. Entire sock is done in twined knitting.

CUFF

Using "Two-Strand Twisted German Cast On" (page 10), with MC on thumb and CC on index finger, CO 60 sts.

Rnd 1: *TK1 MC, TK1 CC; rep from * around.

Rnd 2: *TP1 MC, TP1 CC; rep from * around.

Rnd 3: TK1 MC, RLI CC, *TK1 CC, TK1 MC; rep from * around—61 sts.

Rnds 4–8: TK in small check.

Rnd 9: Alternating MC and CC, TP to 2 sts from end, TP2tog—60 sts.

LEG

Rnd 10: With 1 MC strand, knit around.

Rnds 11–30: Work leg chart. On first rnd, pm every 12 sts between 5 patt reps.

Rnd 31: Rep rnd 10, until 1 st from end, RLI, TK1—61 sts.

Rnds 32–41: TK in small check.

GUSSET

Work gusset in simple stripe.

Move 1 st from needle 2 to needle 1. Needle 1 (instep) has 31 sts arranged as 4 sts, marker, 23 sts, marker, 4 sts. Needle 2 has 30 sts—61 sts total.

Work incs as for basic sock until there are 14 sts before first marker and 14 sts after second marker, with 23 sts between markers. Needle 1 has 51 sts; needle 2 has 30 sts—81 sts total.

HEEL TURN

Work heel turn in small check on center 23 sts between markers.

BEGINNING OF SOLE

Join incs to sole in simple stripe.

FOOT

TK 25 rnds in simple stripe, or until foot measures 2½" less than desired total foot length.

TOE

Work toe in simple stripe.

Second sock: If desired, shift heel to needle 2, so patt jog falls inside ankle on both socks.

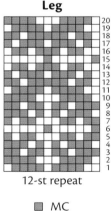

Leg

12-st repeat

■ MC
□ CC

BERRY MEDLEY SOCKS

This "painted" yarn coordinates with its slipper partner (Pink Compass Slippers on page 35). It's the easiest sock design with two yarns and is stranded to bring out the dominance of the painted yarn. By using a solid purple yarn in the nondominant position, the berry colors surface in stripes. Stranding tends to shrink the knitting in the lateral direction. It's important to knit a gauge swatch in the round.

SKILL LEVEL: *Experienced* ●■■▶

SHOE SIZE: *Women's 7/8*

MATERIALS

MC 1 skein of Heritage 150 Paints Sock Yarn from Cascade Yarns (75% merino superwash wool, 25% nylon; 5.25 oz/150 g; 492 yds/450 m) in color 9804 pinks (**2**)

CC 1 skein of Heritage 150 Sock Yarn from Cascade Yarns (75% merino superwash wool, 25% nylon; 5.25 oz/150 g; 492 yds/450 m) in color 5605 purple (**2**)

2 size 4 (3.5 mm) circular needles (16" or 24" long)

14 stitch markers

Tapestry needle

GAUGE: *17 sts and 14 rnds = 2" in stranded simple stripe*

PATTERN

Small Check (page 22)

Simple Stripe (page 22)

Follow the "Basic Sock Pattern" on page 62, noting the specific instructions for each part of the sock. The cuff is twined, while the rest is stranded.

CUFF

Using "Two-Strand Twisted German Cast On" (page 10), with MC on index finger and CC on thumb, CO 61 sts.

Twine knit first 4 rnds of cuff for more stretch.

Rnd 1: TK1 MC, *TK1 CC, TK1 MC; rep from * around.

Rnd 2: TP1 CC, *TP1 MC, TP1 CC; rep from * around.

Rnds 3 and 4: Rep rnds 1 and 2.

Rnds 5–9: Strand knit in small check.

Rnd 10: Strand purl in simple stripe to last 2 sts, TP2tog—60 sts.

LEG

Work in simple stripe for 30 rnds, stranding so that MC is dominant (under CC).

GUSSET

Work gusset in simple stripe.

Move 1 st from needle 2 to needle 1. Needle 1 (instep) has 31 sts arranged as 4 sts, marker, 23 sts, marker, 4 sts. Needle 2 (instep) has 29 sts—60 sts total.

Work incs on needle 1 (heel) until there are 14 sts before first marker and 14 sts after second marker, with 23 sts between markers. Needle 1 has 51 sts; needle 2 has 29 sts—80 sts total.

HEEL TURN

After completing gusset increases, move markers on needle 1 as follows: 13 sts, marker, 25 sts, marker, 13 sts. Work heel turn on center 25 sts in small check.

BEGINNING OF SOLE

Join incs to sole in simple stripe.

FOOT

Strand knit 25 rnds in simple stripe, or until foot measures 2½" less than desired total foot length.

TOE

Work toe in simple stripe.

Second sock: If desired, shift heel to needle 2, so patt jog falls inside ankle on both socks.

WHEEL-OF-HEARTS SOCKS

 Yummy-looking coordinates to their slipper counterparts on page 38, these socks might induce a chocolate-mint craving while you're knitting them. They're twine knit throughout.

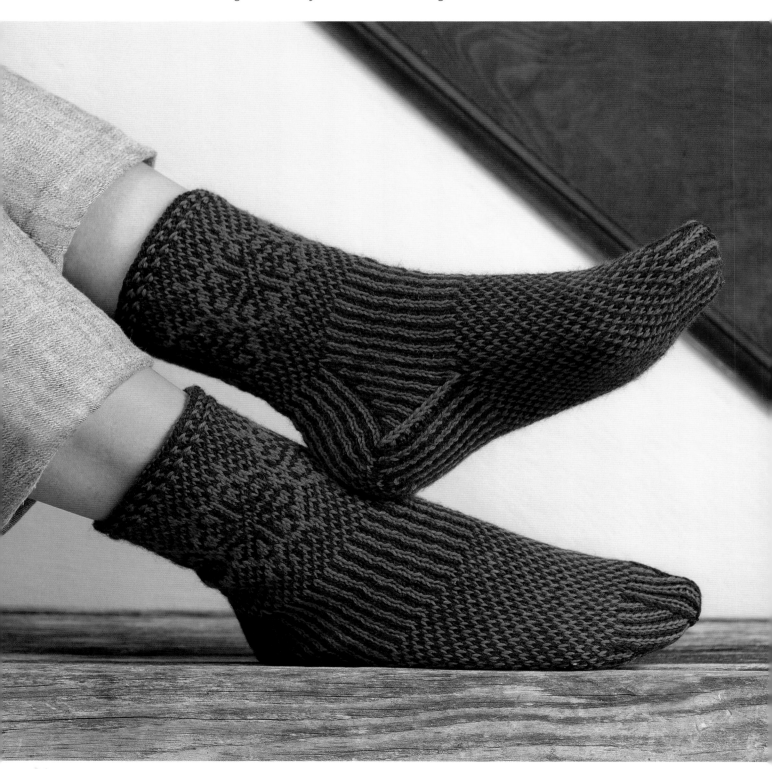

SKILL LEVEL: *Experienced* ●■■▶

SHOE SIZE: *Women's 7/8, Men's 6/7*

MATERIALS

Heritage 150 Sock Yarn from Cascade Yarns (75% super-wash merino wool, 25% nylon; 5.25 oz/150 g; 492 yds/450 m) (**2**)

MC   1 skein in color 5609 brown

CC   1 skein in color 5627 turquoise

2 size 4 (3.5 mm) circular needles (16" or 24" long)

14 stitch markers

Tapestry needle

GAUGE: *15 sts and 14 rnds = 2" in twined knitting*

PATTERNS

Small Check (page 22)

Leg chart

Simple Stripe (page 22

Follow the "Basic Sock Pattern" on page 62, noting the specific instructions for each part of the sock.

CUFF

Using "Two-Strand Twisted German Cast On" (page 10), with MC on thumb and CC on index finger, CO 65 sts.

Rnd 1: TK1 MC, *TK1 CC, TK1 MC; rep from * around.

Rnd 2: TP1 CC, *TP1 MC, TP1 CC; rep from * around.

Rnds 3 and 4: Rep rnds 1 and 2.

LEG

TK 5 rnds in small check. On last rnd TK to last 2 sts, TK2tog—64 sts.

Rnd 1: Work rnd 1 of leg chart, pm every 16 sts between 4 patt reps.

Rnds 2–21: TK to end of chart. On last rnd, work to end of rnd, RLI—65 sts.

TK 5 rnds in small check.

GUSSET

TK gusset in simple stripe as follows.

Rnd 1

Needle 1: (TK1 CC, TK1 MC) twice, pm, *TK1 CC, TK1 MC; rep from * to 5 sts from end; TK1 CC, pm; (TK1 MC, TK1 CC) twice—33 sts.

Needle 2: *TK1 MC, TK1 CC; rep from * around— 32 sts.

Rnd 2: Work both needles even.

Cont with gusset on page 63.

HEEL TURN

After completing gusset incs, work heel turn in small check on center 25 sts.

BEGINNING OF SOLE

Join incs to sole in simple stripe.

FOOT

TK 25 rnds in simple stripe, or until foot measures 2½" less than desired total foot length. On last rnd, divide sts into 6 sections as follows: *11 sts, pm, 10 sts, pm, 11 sts, pm; rep from * to end of needle 2—64 sts total.

TOE

Work toe in simple stripe. To make toe decs fall in the MC sts, move 1 st from needle 1 to needle 2 and start the rnd with a CC st.

Cont toe dec until 5 sts, marker, 4 sts, marker, 5 sts on each needle.

Next rnd

Needle 1: TK2tog, TK1, (TK2tog) 4 times, TK1, TK2tog—8 sts.

Needle 2: Rep needle 1.

Last rnd

Needle 1: Sl 1-TK2tog-psso, TK2tog, TK2tog, sl 1-TK2tog-psso—4 sts.

Needle 2: Rep needle 1.

Second sock: If desired, shift heel to needle 2, so patt jog falls inside ankle on both socks.

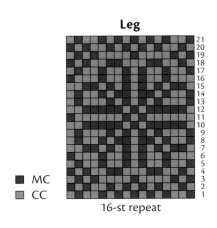

Leg

21 20 19 18 17 16 15 14 13 12 11 10 9 8 7 6 5 4 3 2 1

■ MC
■ CC

16-st repeat

OPTICAL ILLUSION SOCKS

 This pattern is popular in the Nordic countries, and there are many variations of the design. The asymmetrical pattern and high-contrast colors make the illusions pop. This design looks best when twined. For the companion slipper project, see page 41.

SKILL LEVEL: *Experienced* ●●■▶

SHOE SIZE: *Women's 7/8, Men's 6/7*

MATERIALS

Heritage 150 Sock Yarn from Cascade Yarns (75% superwash merino wool, 25% nylon; 5.25 oz/150 g; 492 yds/450 m) (2)

MC 1 skein in color 5601 black

CC 1 skein in color 5618 off-white

2 size 4 (3.5 mm) circular needles (16" or 24" long)

14 stitch markers

Tapestry needle

GAUGE: *16 sts and 14 rows = 2" in optical illusion patt*

PATTERNS

Leg and Instep chart (page 76)

Sole Stripe chart (page 76)

Simple Stripe (page 22)

Follow the "Basic Sock Pattern" on page 62, noting the specific instructions for each part of the sock.

CUFF

Using "Two-Strand Twisted German Cast On" (page 10), with MC on thumb and CC on index finger, CO 64 sts.

Rnd 1: *TK1 MC, TK1 CC; rep from * around.

Rnd 2: *TP1 MC, TP1 CC; rep from * around.

Rnd 3: With 2 strands MC, TK with MC *over*.

Rnd 4: With 2 strands MC, TK with MC *under*.

Rnds 5–8: Rep rnds 3 and 4 twice.

LEG

Rnd 1: Work rnd 1 of leg and instep chart and pm every 8 sts between 8 patt reps.

Rnds 2–28: Cont leg and instep chart.

GUSSET

Incs are made on needle 1 (heel) and worked over even number of sts in simple stripe. Center 25 sts on this needle will become heel. Needle 2 (instep) is worked in leg and instep patt as established.

On alternate inc rnds, 2 sts of same color will be side by side.

Establish stripe patt on needle 1 as follows.

Rnd 1

Needle 1: (TK1 CC, TK1 MC) twice, pm, *TK1 CC, TK1 MC; rep from * to 6 sts from end of needle 1, TK2tog CC, pm, (TK1 MC, TK1 CC) twice—31 sts arranged as 4 sts, marker, 23 sts, marker, 4 sts.

Needle 2: Cont 4 reps of leg and instep chart.

Rnd 2

Needle 1: *TK1 CC, TK1 MC; rep from * to end of needle, slipping markers.

Needle 2: Cont leg and instep chart.

Rnd 3

Needle 1: TK1 CC, TK1 MC, TK1 CC, RLI MC, TK1 MC, slip marker, *TK1 CC, TK1 MC; rep from * to 1 st before next marker, TK1 CC, slip marker, TK1 MC, LLI MC, TK1 CC, TK1 MC, TK1 CC.

Note: On rnds 4, 8, 12, 16, and 20, make RLI and LLI with CC.

Needle 2: Cont leg and instep chart.

Rnd 4

Needle 1: Cont in simple stripe.

Needle 2: Cont leg and instep chart.

Rep rnds 3 and 4 until there are 14 sts before first marker and 14 sts after second marker, with 23 sts between markers. Needle 1 has 51 sts; needle 2 has 32 sts—83 sts total.

HEEL TURN

After completing gusset incs, move markers on needle 1 as follows: 13 sts, marker, 25 sts, marker, 13 sts. Work heel turn on center 25 sts in small check.

BEGINNING OF SOLE

Join incs to sole in simple stripe. Cont leg and instep chart on needle 2.

FOOT

Work 28 rnds on heel (needle 1) of sole stripe chart, and 28 rnds on instep (needle 2) of leg and instep chart. The patt on sole draws in a little, snugging foot and making it thicker.

On last rnd, divide sts into 6 sections as follows: *11 sts, pm, 10 sts, pm, 11 sts; rep from * to end for needle 2—64 sts.

TOE

Work top of toe in leg and instep chart, and bottom of toe in simple stripe. To make toe decs fall in MC sts, move 1 st from needle 1 to needle 2 and start rnd with CC st.

Cont toe dec until you have 5 sts, marker, 4 sts, marker, 5 sts on each needle.

Next rnd

Needle 1: TK2tog, TK1, (TK2tog) 4 times, TK1, TK2tog—8 sts.

Needle 2: Rep needle 1.

Last rnd

Needle 1: Sl 1-TK2tog-psso, TK2tog, TK2tog, sl 1-TK2tog-psso—4 sts.

Needle 2: Rep needle 1.

Second sock: If desired, shift heel to needle 2, so patt jog falls inside ankle on both socks.

Leg and Instep

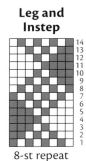

8-st repeat

Sole Stripe

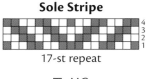

17-st repeat

■ MC
□ CC

Slip your socks into their companion slippers for a coordinated pair.

Yellow Pansy Socks

Spring is in the air! These socks are great to show off in clogs. The yarn is hard-wearing bamboo, but feels like butter. To optimize stretch and wearability, the socks are twine knit in some areas and stranded in others. The companion slippers can be found on page 44.

SKILL LEVEL: *Experienced* ●■■⬤

SHOE SIZE: *Women's 9/10*

MATERIALS

Pediboo from Frog Tree Yarns (80% washable merino wool, 20% bamboo; 3.5 oz/100 g; 255 yds/ 200 m) **4**

> **MC** 1 skein in color 1197 pink
>
> **CC** 1 skein in color 1193 yellow

2 size 4 (3.5 mm) circular needles (16" or 24" long)

14 stitch markers

Tapestry needle

GAUGE: *15 sts and 15 rnds = 2" in twined zigzag small check*

PATTERNS

Basket chart

Flower chart

Small Check (page 22)

Zigzag Simple Stripe (page 22)

Zigzag Small Check in the Round (page 22)

Follow the "Basic Sock Pattern" on page 62, noting the specific instructions for each part of the sock.

CUFF

Using "Two-Strand Twisted German Cast On" (page 10), with MC on thumb and CC on index finger, CO 60 sts.

Rnd 1: *TK1 MC, TK1 CC; rep from * around.

Rnd 2: *TP1 MC, TP1 CC; rep from * around.

Rnds 3–8: TK in zigzag simple stripe.

LEG

Rnd 1: TK rnd 1 of basket chart, pm every 12 sts for 5 reps.

Rnds 2–13: TK basket chart to end.

Rnd 14: With 1 strand MC, knit.

Rnds 15–25: TK 11 rnds of flower chart.

Rnd 26: With 1 strand MC, K1, M1, knit to end of rnd—61 sts.

GUSSET

On inc rnds, 2 same-color sts will be side by side. On next inc rnd, place other color inc between them.

Rnd 1: TK even in zigzag small check.

Rnd 2

Needle 1 (heel): TK 2, RLI, TK1, pm, knit to 3 sts from end of needle 1, pm, TK1, LLI, TK2—32 sts.

Needle 2 (instep): TK even in patt—31 sts.

Rnd 3: TK even in patt.

Rep rnds 2 and 3 until 13 sts before first marker, and 13 sts after second marker, with 24 sts in between. Needle 1 has 50 sts; needle 2 has 31 sts—81 sts total.

HEEL TURN

Work heel turn on center 24 sts in small check.

BEGINNING OF SOLE

Join incs to sole and TK in regular small check. Cont zigzag small check on needle 2.

FOOT

TK small check on sole (needle 1) and TK zigzag small check on instep (needle 2). Work patts for 24 rnds, or until foot measures 2½" less than desired total foot length.

TOE

Work toe in small check on needle 1 and zigzag small check on needle 2. When dec, 2 lps of same color will fall next to each other. They'll be knit tog in a later rnd.

Cut strands leaving a 6" tail. Pull MC through rem lps and tighten. Weave in yarn ends.

Basket

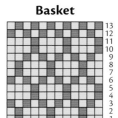

12-st repeat

Flower

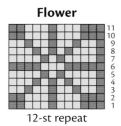

12-st repeat

■ MC
□ CC

Abbreviations and Glossary

beg	begin(ning)
BO	bind off
CC	contrasting color
CO	cast on
cont	continue(ing)(s)
dec(s)	decrease(ing)(s)
dpn(s)	double-pointed needle(s)
g	gram(s)
inc(s)	increase(ing)(s)
K	knit (regular)
K2tog	knit 2 stitches together—1 stitch decreased
kw	knitwise
LH	left hand
LLI	left-lifted increase (see page 18)
lp(s)	loop(s)
M1	make 1 stitch (see page 18)
MC	main color
m	meter
mm	millimeter(s)
oz	ounce(s)
P	purl (regular)
patt(s)	pattern(s)
pm	place marker
psso	pass slipped stitch over
PU	pick up and knit
pw	purlwise
rem	remain(ing)
rep(s)	repeat(ing)(s)
RH	right hand
RLI	right-lifted increase (see page 18)
rnd(s)	round(s)
RS	right side
sk	skip
sl	slip
sl 1	slip 1 stitch purlwise with yarn in back unless otherwise instructed
sl st(s)	slip stitch(es)—slip stitches purlwise unless instructed otherwise
SSTK	twined knit decrease (see page 19)
st(s)	stitch(es)
St st(s)	stockinette stitch(es)
tbl	through back loop(s)
tog	together
TK	twine knit
TP	twine purl
TK2tog	twine knit 2 stitches together (see page 19)
TP2tog	twine purl 2 stitches together (see page 19)
WS	wrong side
wyib	with yarn in back
wyif	with yarn in front
yd(s)	yards

Resources

Cascade Yarns
www.cascadeyarns.com

Cascade 220
Cascade 220 Superwash
Cascade 220 Superwash Paints
Cascade 220 Superwash Sport
Heritage 150 Sock Yarn
Heritage 150 Paints Sock Yarn
Pastaza

Frog Tree Yarns
www.frogtreeyarns.com

Pediboo

Westing Bridge
www.chiaogoo.com

9" ChiaoGoo Circular Bamboo Needles

USEFUL INFORMATION

STANDARD YARN WEIGHTS

Yarn-Weight Symbol and Category Name	1 Super Fine	2 Fine	3 Light	4 Medium	5 Bulky	6 Super Bulky
Types of Yarn in Category	Sock, Finger-ing, Baby	Sport, Baby	DK, Light Worsted	Worsted, Afghan, Aran	Chunky, Craft, Rug	Bulky, Roving
Knit Gauge Range* in Stockinette Stitch to 4"	27 to 32 sts	23 to 26 sts	21 to 24 sts	16 to 20 sts	12 to 15 sts	6 to 11 sts
Recommended Needle in U.S. Size Range	1 to 3	3 to 5	5 to 7	7 to 9	9 to 11	11 and larger
Recommended Needle in Metric Size Range	2.25 to 3.25 mm	3.25 to 3.75 mm	3.75 to 4.5 mm	4.5 to 5.5 mm	5.5 to 8 mm	8 mm and larger

These are guidelines only. The above reflect the most commonly used gauges and needle or hook sizes for specific yarn categories.

SKILL DIFFICULTY

If you're fairly new to knitting, I suggest you practice first. Soon you'll be ready for the challenge of the projects rated "experienced."

◼☐☐☐ Beginner: Projects for first-time knitters using basic knit and purl stitches. Minimal shaping.

◼◼☐☐ Easy: Projects using basic stitches, repetitive stitch patterns, and simple color changes, shaping, and finishing.

◼◼◼☐ Intermediate: Projects using a variety of stitches, such as basic cables and lace, simple intarsia, and techniques for double-pointed needles and knitting in the round. Mid-level shaping and finishing.

◼◼◼◼ Experienced: Projects using advanced techniques and stitches, such as short rows, Fair Isle, more intricate intarsia, cables, lace patterns, and numerous color changes.

METRIC CONVERSION

m	=	yds	x	0.9144
yds	=	m	x	1.0936
g	=	oz	x	28.35
oz	=	g	x	0.0352